JOY
for the
Journey

The Royal Road in
Time of Distress

Rev. Robert
Mendonca

Print ISBN: 978-1-09831-805-5

eBook ISBN: 978-1-09831-806-2

To Phylis Linton, who practices and shares joy every day.

CONTENTS

Foreword..1

Chapter 1: Glad Tidings, Great Joy..3

Chapter 2: The Old Testament: The Call to Joy.............................9

Chapter 3: The New Testament: The Joy Fulfilled.........................18

Chapter 4: Kill Joys...28

Chapter 5: Joy and Happiness...37

Chapter 6: Baptism in the Holy Spirit..42

Chapter 7: The Royal Road to Joy...54

Chapter 8: The Way, Truth, and Life..62

Chapter 9: Prayer, Temptation, and Sin along the Road...............70

Chapter 10: Joy and the Prayer Meeting...77

Chapter 11: Walking the Royal Road in
Times of Worldwide Challenge..86

Glossary...93

Endnotes..103

Bibliography..107

FOREWORD

Many years ago I opened the magazine *Commonweal* to see a group picture of the U.S. Catholic Bishops. Their faces expressed the weight of the world, or pessimism about the problems of the world. These eighty or so men were standing under a banner that proclaimed "Share Our **Joy**!" For years, this incongruity has struck me as incompatible with the message of the Gospel, that of joy in the Lord. This lack of Christian joy seemed to be a central problem to many Christians. It is a real hindrance to evangelization. Lack of joy often leads to falling prey to temptation.

We seem to be overwhelmed. Even many of our charismatic prayer groups seem to be routine, lacking joy. Is there something missing? Perhaps we have yet to receive the Baptism of the Holy Spirit. Maybe we are overwhelmed by the events happening is the world—the violence, the lack of moral true north, the threat of epidemics. The invasion of COVID-19 hasn't changed the Christian message and mission, but has honed it.

This book will explore the road and the journey through which we live and move and have our being. And language is central to our walk. Behind the English translation of the scriptures is the Greek language, and behind the Greek is Hebrew. Most of us don't have a basic understanding of Greek and Hebrew, and modern Bible translation is to varying degrees based on earlier translations. Meanings of English words have changed greatly since Shakespeare's day. For this reason I have included a glossary of Greek and Hebrew words at the end of this book. When you come across a word in boldface type, it indicates an entry in the glossary.

What is joy? How is it different from happiness? How can I keep it in good times and in bad? What does God's word say about it? And, above all, how can I find it? This book will examine the necessity and importance of Christian joy, and how joy is God's sign and His gift.

There is a royal road to joy and peace, a road that—while it may not be easy—is direct. The royal road is focused and is a real means of survival and triumph over our invisible enemy. We will now embark on a journey on that royal road in the Spirit. For many of us, this will be a resumption of the path to peace and joy in the Lord; for others, it will be a major revelation and invitation to journey with and through the Lord Jesus Christ. These were my thoughts when I began writing this book late in 2019. Today we find ourselves in a struggle, not only with the ancient spiritual forces of evil but also with the novel COVID-19 virus. We fight the physical spread of the invader. We fight fear and despair. Where recently we could attend church services, now we find ourselves sheltering in place. This book includes many events from my life; events of kindness, stories of selflessness, and even danger underpin the scriptures and conversation along the royal road. It is my prayer that during these times where families are sequestered they may share important stories, which their children will hand on to their children long after these painful days are gone.

CHAPTER ONE

GLAD TIDINGS, GREAT JOY

Searching for and finding lasting joy is difficult in ordinary times, but in times such as these—where the news is loaded with universal sorrows, where people are wondering about the present and the future, where all that had seemed so important only days ago now is seen against the backdrop of the Coronavirus and life-and-death challenges of fear and uncertainty—it is a very difficult task. Joy can be the handmaid to our spiritual survival and even prospering, finding new ways to relate to family, spouse, and children.

Where are we to search for this joy? What model can we seek? I think the intertwining of our life stories with the greatest story ever told, the Incarnation, is the way to proceed. It is to Christmas time that we will first search for our model for Christian joy.

I was married for twenty-four years prior to my ordination. Lori and I had a wonderful marriage, but in all of our married life, she only had two years of health; and these occurred as short episodes scattered over the life of the marriage. Lori was a victim of systemic lupus erythematosus, a disease in which the body produces antibodies attacking its own organs. We had great joy and love amid her pain and suffering. Sometimes I felt very tired, working two jobs, going to university, shopping and cooking. I was a caregiver. I have had many jobs and have many interests. Most of my life I made my living as a musician. This included almost forty years as director of music ministries at various churches. When I met Lori, I was a conservatory student, hanging around with a group of composers and artists. I was a blasphemer, and Lori brought me back to Christ. I finally got my teaching credentials. It was in this way that I found myself teaching band and choir in a public school.

It was many years ago, around Christmas time. I was teaching at Alvarado Middle School in Union City, California. It too was a year of tragedy. We had already experienced the death of one beloved teacher. The school had barely recovered from that, when we heard that a former student of mine had died on a basketball court at Logan High School. He was a freshman. "Jed," as we will call him, had played the piano in my concert band. His legs didn't reach the pedals; he had to sit on phone books.

Jed's life had already been a miracle. He was born with a hole in his heart. At that time such a condition was inoperable. The doctors told his parents that Jed would have a life expectancy of about five years. He lived to the age of fourteen.

The school sent me as an official representative to Jed's funeral. My heart and the very air of that Advent evening were filled with anguish, even though I knew that Jed was with the

Lord. As long as I live, I shall never forget the wailing of his mother. This, combined with loss of a dear friend and faculty member, Lori's suffering, and my own self-pity contributed to a burden of grief. I had to stop at the mall to shop for dinner. I was depressed.

Then I heard it. It was a quartet of singers. The air was filled with music: "O Little Town of Bethlehem" and "Silent Night." I asked them if I could join in, and they gave me a songbook. The air grew less cold; my heart was filled with hope and wonder and thanksgiving—and, yes, **joy**! I returned home with peace in the midst of that cold, sad Advent.

The great pastor, theologian and martyr, Dietrich Bonhoeffer, once said "Music...will help dissolve your perplexities and purify your character and sensibilities, and in time of care and sorrow, will keep a fountain of joy alive in you."[1] How true it was that night when the events of the day were swallowed up in joy! Among times and seasons, it is perhaps Christmas that has the most joy built into it. This is true even if we don't regularly feel that joy. I suggest we begin our joyful journey with the Christmas season. Before we look at the sacred scripture, let's look into what's going on here.

Christmas is indeed a good time to begin our quest for joy. It was 1978 and Lori and I moved from San Francisco to Alameda, California, where I took the position of Director of Music Ministries. Because of Lori's physical condition, the move was very difficult—even though it was only across the Bay Bridge. These were changing times. These were also times of challenge. In August, Pope John Paul I died suddenly and mysteriously.

On November 18, Jim Jones of the People's Temple had just killed Congressman Leo Ryan and left for dead his assistant, Jackie Speier.[2] She later filled Ryan's congressional seat in 2008. Strangely, when I had a public relations agency in San Francisco, members of Jones' People's Temple sought my professional services. My family and I were protected from this cult. It had been a crazy year. A little over a week after the Jonestown massacre San Francisco mayor George Moscone, and a county supervisor, Harvey Milk, were assassinated by Dan White, another county supervisor. It was against that crazy quilt of horror that Lori and I moved to Saint Barnabas parish in Alameda. All these things were going on sequentially and simultaneously!

Preparation for Christmas took up most of the time between late November and Christmas. The move had taken all our money. We hardly knew anyone in the parish. We had no money left for a Christmas dinner or a Christmas tree or even the smallest Christmas gift for one another. We were ready to sleep early when our doorbell rang. It was Gerry and Gloria, choir members—our first friends in the parish. They brought a Christmas tree. They brought some food, saying they had some leftovers from their dinner. They even brought some presents for Lori and me! Among the exhaustion and the horror of what was coming down in the Bay area and in Guyana, our new friends had provided a Christmas of love and joy!

Numerous Christmas and Advent songs bid us to rejoice. We are told to rejoice because Emanuel will come to Israel. We ask God to "rest us merry." The real music of Christmas—by that I mean music that somehow reflects the reason for the season—is not all an admonition to joy. Two other themes dominate the wonderful music of Christmas: glory and variations on the historical theme of God becoming man. Some on these celebrate the holy irony of the Baby born in a feeding trough, exposed to the cold night air, the king of the universe in abject poverty. These then are the main themes of true Christmas music.

Christmas joy is centered on the birth of Jesus, the joy of family and belonging, the joy of gathering together with friends, kindness, gift-giving, and receiving food and music. These things come together in a unique blend that makes the Christmas holidays a perfect medium for us to begin to understand joy. In more general terms, this joy is about belonging, being moved by music, dance, and shared meals. We shall search the sacred scriptures for these categories.

There are some problems with this approach that I propose: Christmas joy seems to be more a cause of happiness rather than joy. Happiness is based on circumstances. Joy is not. Christian and biblical joy is grounded in the truth that the Lord has come in the flesh, that He died for our sins, rose for our justification, and has adopted us as His sons and daughters. Of course those are circumstances, but they are things that do not change.

When the source of our joy is based on our current situation, our joy is very transitory. This accounts for some of the much-touted notion of the Christmas depression. The paradigm of Christmas joy arises from circumstances. Do we have family? Do we have fellowship? Or are we isolated at this time of year? Does the music ring hollow on the ear? Do I associate the season with personal loss? So our joy can disappear in a flash. Yet the elements that make up the joy we experience at Christmas are the same elements that spring out of worship, the fact God has broken in to history and that family, friends, music, and the other elements of Eucharistic banquet sing eloquently to our hearts. Joy in Christ is paralleled in the joys of Christmas. We will come to see that Christian joy is like so many children's toys: "Some assembly is required."

CHAPTER TWO

THE OLD TESTAMENT: THE CALL TO JOY

From our Christmas holidays we have an idea of what joy looks like and sounds like. We have discussed some of the conditions that make for what we might call circumstantial joy. Even when the occasion of our joy has a religious basis, if the joy is circumstantial, it can go away when the first gloomy day or loss occurs. In dark times we need the light more than usual, so let us begin to see what the Hebrew scriptures say about joy.

There are several words in Hebrew that can be translated as "**rejoice**" or "joy." We will examine some of these words and passages that were the first to call Jews and Christians to joy.

One of the first references to joy in God's word relates to the three great pilgrims feasts. In Deuteronomy we encounter rejoicing in the context of festive worship. *Samach* indicates a joy that is both spontaneous and of extreme gladness. Dancing, singing and music sometimes accompany it. This is a far cry from singing "Joyful, Joyful We Adore Thee" with faces full of sorrow and defeat. Chapter 16 of *Deuteronomy* speaks of Passover (Pesach), Pentecost (Shavu'ot) and Booths or Tabernacles (Sukkot or Sukkos). There is a trend among some Christians to celebrate these feasts today. Indeed, many churches celebrate the Seder, the Passover feast. But the whole is preserved in the Catholic, Orthodox, Lutheran, and Anglican traditions as Eucharist or The Lord's Supper. We rejoice that Christ, our Passover is slain. We celebrate Christ's resurrection from the dead as first fruits. Therefore we too rejoice in so great a salvation. This, of course, is the main reason for our joy.

We begin our meditation by reading Deuteronomy 16:11, 14-15. What do we find here? Joy! Yes, Deuteronomy is a God-breathed invitation to joy. While the name of the book in Greek means second law (*D'varim* in Hebrew),[3] the book contains way more than rules and regulations. Amid the three sermons of Moses and regulations for worship, there is (wait for it) Joy!

Joy is also very prevalent in the feast of Pentecost. Orthodox and Conservative Jews observe it for two days. Although many dates have been observed for the celebration of Feast of Weeks (Pentecost), it is celebrated seven weeks after Passover. Synagogues and homes are decked out with greenery. It began as a grain harvest festival, but after time became a celebration of the giving of the Torah, the Law, and by extension the whole Bible. Deuteronomy tells the people of God to rejoice not only over the harvest, but also the harvest that would come because of God's holy Word.

For Christians, the joy continues. As the giving of the Law was commemorated on Pentecost, so the Holy Church was born in the profound power of the Holy Spirit. This became the center of the Charismatic gifts—indeed, an occasion of joy for all Christians.

But by far the longest and most joyful of these great feasts is the Feast of Tabernacles (*Sukkos*). It is one feast that was never taken over from Judaism to Christianity. Some Jews celebrate *Sukkos* for nine days; others observe just a week. During this time the people live outdoors. They are loaded with joy, a joy that we have every reason to emulate.

Through the years, these pilgrim feasts eventually became occasions for the singing of the Psalms known as the Songs of Ascent. The Christian tradition calls them Gradual Psalms (Psalms 120–134). The exact origin of titles of these is not known. Some have suggested that they relate to fifteen stairs in the temple from which these were sung. Others maintain that these psalms had melodies that rose incrementally from low to high. It is also said these Psalms were sung on return from exile during the time of Ezra. Ultimately the pilgrims sang them when coming up to Jerusalem for the Pilgrim Feasts.[4] Jerusalem is higher than the surrounding countryside, so pilgrims always ascended to the Holy City.

Since these Psalms prepared the pilgrims for the joy of the feasts, should we not also pray them in our quest for joy in the Lord? Should we not sing or read them as we go up from sadness to gladness? Should they not accompany us as an inducement to rejoice—even in persecution? Should we not recite them as we battle the worldwide COVID-19? If these Psalms are great teachers of joy, repentance, and constancy during times of trouble, how much more are they helpful to us at all times. The Psalms are a school of joy, a *schola gaudium*. "I was glad when they said to me, 'Let us go to the house of the Lord!' Our feet are standing within your gates, O Jerusalem" (Psalm 122).

It was such a joy to recite this psalm as I visited Jerusalem. It was back in the 1990s. Saddam Hussein was attempting to shoot Russian-made missiles at Israel from Iraq. I suffered an accidental fall at the Sea of Galilee. But the Psalm brought me such a joy that I quickly forget the worries about incoming missiles (albeit it out of range) and the pain from my fall. It was the joy of the Lord! Let's look at a few of the uses of words translated as "joy." In *First Samuel* 18:6 we encounter David coming home from killing Goliath, the Philistine, and the women coming out rejoicing with tambourines and songs of joy. Here we see the joy of victory celebrated with music. The same word, *samakh*, is used as King Solomon is anointed king. The people blew the trumpet as the crowds shouted, "Long live King Solomon." So the people followed the king "playing on pipes and rejoicing with great joy, so that the earth quaked at their noise" (1 Kings 1:40).

Another important aspect of joy begins strangely enough with a lamentation for sin and guilt. Psalm 51 begins with a lament for sin, as King David begs God for the application of His mercy. It is time for him and us to be completely washed from sin. The psalm is very dark, but at verse 8 this characteristic begins to morph to bright promises. We go from sin, condemnation and guilt to joy and gladness. "Let me hear joy and gladness;

let the bones you have crushed rejoice. Hide your face from my sins, and blot out all my iniquities" (Psalm 51:8-9).

How does this psalm lead us from sin and guilt to joy? First we must look at the picture that God, artist that He is, paints in Psalm 51. The heading reads as follows: "For the leader. A psalm of David, when the prophet Nathan came to him, after he had gone into Bathsheba."

Remember the details of this portrait? David burned with passion for Bathsheba, wife of Uriah, David's armor-bearer. David became totally smitten with Bathsheba as she was bathing. The king committed adultery with her. She became pregnant. This began a chain of events. The king devised a plan to send Uriah home to sleep with his wife in order that when David's child would be born, no one would suspect the king of adultery. Just to remind you, although Uriah went home, he did not sleep with Bathsheba. To understand the setting of Psalm 51, you must take a moment now to read *Second Samuel*, chapter 11. David orders that Uriah should be cut off in battle and killed by the enemy.

In *Second Samuel*, chapter 12, we hear Nathan's condemnation of David using the story of two men in a town. Take another moment to read Nathan's words ending with his strong pronouncement, "You are the man!" (2 Samuel 12:7). It is right after these words that the king begins, "Have mercy on me, O God, according to your steadfast love." In the first part of Psalm 51 we encounter the extremity of guilt for sin. In David's case, adultery led to murder. But David was eventually led by repentance to joy and gladness. He speaks of the bones, which were crushed. Bear in mind, these bones are not merely broken; they are smashed.[5]

Sometimes our lives seem smashed, our dreams obliterated, and we feel oppressed in every event of our lives. How dare you try to elicit joy in this mess? This is true even as we experience worldwide fear. And yet King David saw no incongruity in experiencing pain, guilt, and judgment while also experiencing joy. As Kahlil Gibran (1883–1931), the noted Christian poet and artist, said, "Your joy is your sorrow unmasked. Is not the cup that holds your wine the very cup that was burned in the potter's oven?6 One reason given for joy and gladness in the Bible is that God forgives sins. If this is true for the Hebrew Scriptures, how much more applicable for those who follow the Lord Jesus!

We see yet another reason for joy and gladness in the *Book of Esther*. It is similar to Psalm 51, namely deliverance from persecution and salvation from mass destruction. *Esther* chapter 8 presents a joy so intense it must be mentioned here. Haman, the highest advisor to the Persian king, felt insulted by Mordecai, a Jew and cousin of Esther. The wicked advisor plots the extermination of the Jews. Esther has become queen while keeping her Jewishness a secret from the king. As a masterful stroke, Queen Esther denounces Haman in the presence of her husband, King Ahasuerus. Haman then is hanged on the very gallows on which Mordecai was to be hanged!

There is a reversal of fortunes. This is a common theme throughout the Bible. While the biblical tradition is fully enunciated in the New Testament, reversal is present in many sections of the Old Testament. The child of promise of Abraham was not his first-born, Ishmael, but Isaac, Sarah's son (Genesis 21:1-6). There was reversal in the inability of Rebekah to conceive, and after prayer she does. She gives birth to twins Esau and Jacob. A second reversal occurs when Esau sells his birthright for lentil stew. Rebekah engages in deception, but reversal again occurs (Genesis 25:19-34). Hannah's prayer is the model for Mary's *Magnificat:* "The bows of the mighty are broken, but the feeble gird on strength...the barren has borne seven, but she who has many children is forlorn" (1 Samuel 2:4,5b).

Perhaps the most impressive is in the Book of *Esther.* Mordecai emerges from Ahasuerus' palace in royal robes of blue and white, wearing a golden crown. The joy that emerges from this liberation is among the greatest in the Old Testament:

> The city of Susa shouted and rejoiced. For the Jews there was light and gladness, joy and honor. In every province and in every city, wherever the king's command and his edict came, there was gladness and joy among the Jews, a festival and a holiday. Furthermore, many of the peoples of that country professed to be Jews, because the fear of the Jews had fallen upon them (Esther 8: 15b-17).

This great deliverance of the Jewish people became the feast of Purim, a time of feasting and rejoicing. The idea that reversal is in the plan of God can be a great comfort to us. In the midst of affliction and loss we too can experience God's life-changing joy permeating our existence.

The removal of oppression and the reversal of dire situations are designed to lead us to joy and gladness. I argue that this is not the result of some kind of "plan B" on the part of God. To us it looks as if God keeps adapting situations so that things will turn out well. But a few verses in the New Testament should put the plan B scenario to rest. Ephesians 1:4 reminds us that God chose us before the foundation of the world. Revelation 13:8b informs us that believers' names "have been written from the foundation of the world in the book of life of the Lamb that was slaughtered." Before creation, God knew that the human race would need redemption. Another reason for joy is the Lord not only loves us; His plan A was that we should come to faith and salvation in His Son. That certainly is a reason for rejoicing!

Finally, the euphoria on the restoration of Jerusalem, the rebuilding of the holy temple, and the rediscovery of the sacred books that we encounter in the books of *Ezra* and *Nehemiah* are among the greatest outbursts of joy in the whole Old Testament. The repatriation of the Jewish people to their homeland with freedom to worship God, to rebuild the holy temple, and to hear and practice his holy word is the quintessential model for reversal and spiritual joy. Remember so-often-quoted Nehemiah 8:10, "The joy of the Lord is your strength." Again, the context is instructive. Notice how the people worship with their bodies, perhaps reminding us of Paul's in Romans 12 about worshipping God in our mortal bodies.

Ezra opened the book in everyone's sight. He was standing higher than all the others. When Ezra opened the book of the Law, all the people stood up. Next Ezra blessed the people; they lifted up their hands and answered "Amen, amen." Then they bowed their heads and worshipped God with their faces to the ground. Notice how the whole body is involved!

> And Nehemiah, who was the governor, and Ezra the priest and scribe, And the Levites who taught the people said to all the people, "this day is holy to the Lord your God; do not mourn or weep." For all the people wept when they heard the words of the law. Then he said to them, "Go your way, eat fat and drink sweet wine and send portions of them to those for whom nothing is pre-pared, for this day is holy to our Lord; and do not be grieved, for the joy of the Lord is your strength." So the Levites stilled all the people, saying, "be quiet, for this day is holy; do not be grieved." And all the people went their way to eat and drink and to send portions and to make great rejoicing, because they had understood the words that were declared to them (Neh. 8:9-12).

Once again, we encounter this marvelous joy of the Lord, but it is in the context of freedom of worship that all should rejoice. Those who are so blessed to have such freedom must thank God with joy. It is our strength!

CHAPTER THREE

THE NEW TESTAMENT: THE JOY FULFILLED

There are some people who seem to radiate joy. They laugh at disaster; like show people, "they smile when they are low"; they see the world through rose-tinted glasses. In short, there is a natural gift of joy. Some people are able to maintain a positive outlook under almost any circumstances. This is not what we mean by Christian joy. People with a high tolerance for adversity can be difficult to be around. That consistent affect can lead to reacting inappropriately to certain situations. The joy we are talking about is joy that is not situational. It also does not proceed from our natural inclinations or customary attitudes. True joy proceeds from knowing Jesus Christ. For this reason we must follow the necessity of Baptism in the Holy Spirit with how we can receive this vital gift and how it promotes true joy.

Joy is not only a central theme, in the New Covenant, but also a way of life. Jesus himself makes known the connection between following Him and joy, not only joy for the believer, but for the Lord Himself! On the same night that Jesus celebrated Passover with His disciples, Jesus speaks of many important things to the Apostles: He shows how He is the vine and we are the branches; He promises to send the Holy Spirit and He bids us to obey His commandment. He says to His followers for all time: "As the Father has loved me, so I have loved you; abide in my love. If you keep my commandments, you will abide in my love, just as I have kept my Father's commandments and abide in his love. I have said these things to you so that my joy may be in you, and that your joy may be complete" (John 15:9-10).

We have seen how Christmas "joy" is a kind of model for joy in that it turns upon family and friends, for food and drink, music, and gift-giving and receiving. But this is situational. It has to do with the possession of perceived goods. If we don't have them, how can we be joyful? We have seen that in the Old Testament that joy is also situational. Such joy is experienced in deliverance from destruction, on great Jewish feasts, in worship and in hearing God's word proclaimed. Remember, we said that in Christian worship "some assembly is required." This requirement for meeting together is a missing element in the strategy against the current pandemic, so-called sheltering in place. If we are sequestered with others prudently distanced, assembly can be a great help in the home situation.

Yet we must also remember St. Paul's admonition, "For the kingdom of God is not food and drink, but righteousness and peace and joy in the Holy Spirit" (Rom 14:17). In Christ, joy has shifted from being situational to being a way of life. How can we worship in apparent sorrow?

So then on what is Christian joy based? This is extremely simple. It is based on Jesus Christ Himself. The name Jesus is an Anglicized version of **Yeshua**. The name above all names is a combination of a shortened form of what is called the **Tetragrammaton**, the sacred name that spoke from the burning bush to Moses. Jews do not pronounce this name; it is so sacred. It is abbreviated YHWH. It is sometimes translated, as "I am who I am." Alternatively it may be translated, as "I am what I am," or "I will be what I will be." Contained in the **Name** or *HaShem* is the notion of past, present, and future. We see this reflected in the New Testament. In the *Letter to the Hebrews* we read, "Jesus Christ is the same yesterday and today and forever (Heb. 13:8). This is confirmed by the words of Jesus whom John identifies as the one who freed us from our sins, who was pierced and is coming on the clouds: "'I am the Alpha and the Omega,' says the Lord God, who is and who was and who is to come, the Almighty" (Rev. 1:8).[7]

So the first cause for Christian joy is Jesus Himself. He is our joy by the very fact of his existence. In other words he is Lord, One with the Father. He is also Messiah, Christ, Savior! **Messiah** in English has the basic meaning of being anointed with oil. Such anointing takes place for a particular purpose. Although the anointing seems originally associated with the monarchy and priesthood, later such anointing became associated with the prophetic office.[8] Ironically, in the Old Testament the only attribution of the title "messiah" is given to Cyrus, the Persian king the Lord chose to rebuild Jerusalem (Isaiah 45:1).

Years ago when I was visiting Jerusalem, I was having lunch with our guide. I was looking at posters on walls near our eatery. I asked the guide, "Does that say what I think it says?" There was a picture of a Hasidic man. At the bottom of what turned out to be an election poster was the candidate's name with the designation "messiah" in Hebrew! My guide told me it was a common practice to refer to leaders as messiahs.

So it looks like even Christian joy is based on a happening after all. God has broken into history! Christian joy is an attitude; it should be a way of life. In short, Christian joy begins with Christ himself! The writer of *Hebrews* admonishes us to "Look to Jesus the pioneer and **perfector** of our faith, who for the sake of the joy that was set before him endured the cross..." (Heb. 12:2). In trying to understand the joy set before the Lord, we may discover important information. In this passage the author of *Hebrews* refers to the joy that the Lord Jesus gained through the salvation of so many witnesses. Bear in mind that the Greek word for "**witnesses**" is *martyroi*. For the first centuries of Christianity, Christians had to be ready to die for their faith, just as Jesus gave his life for the life of the world.

This brings us to an unexpected corelation between joy and sorrow. This is a very imporant aspect to Christian joy. It is not a joy that discounts suffering and shame. It is a joy that transends the suffering and shame. How can Christians maintain joy when so many things are wrong with the world? The joy for our Savior is in the knowledge that his death would make possible the ultimate triumph over all evil.

Hebrews outlines for us what power proceeds from the Sacrifice of Christ that makes it possible for him to endure the cross—not only the pain, but the shame of the cross as well. Another reason for the Lord's joy, in light of pain and shame, is Jesus taking his seat at the right hand of God! The writer of *Hebrews* reminds us that the saving action, the cause of Jesus' joy, is also "so that you may not grow weary or lose heart" (Heb 12:3b). Theodoret of Cyr (393–457 AD) speaks of the Savior's joy as "the salvation of human beings; for it he endured the suffering"[9]

Another cause for rejoicing is that joy, faith, and endurance are free gifts. St. Augustine (354–430 AD) proclaims what the scripture tells us, that faith and salvation are a free gift from God. "And if faith has led us to the bath of regeneration, we ought not for that reason to think that we have first given something, so that our saving regeneration might be given us in return."[10] We can do nothing to deserve faith or Baptism.

We are given both a command and a methodology for living the Christian life of joy. "Rejoice in the Lord always; again I will say, Rejoice" (Phil. 4:4). If this admonition stopped there, it would seem cryptic or maybe an impossible claim. But St. Paul relates this joy to several other attitudes that can help us to be truly joyful. We are also provided with both remedies to Christian long faces as well as areas where the world attacks our joy and how we can be vulnerable to the Evil One who steals our joy:

Let your ***gentleness*** be known to everyone. *The Lord is near. Do not **worry*** about anything, but in everything by ***prayer*** and Supplication with thanksgiving let your requests be made known to God. And the peace of God, which surpasses all understanding, will ***guard*** your hearts and your minds in Christ Jesus (Phil. 4:5-7, emphasis mine).

A reason and safeguard for our joy is gentleness; Paul uses a word that is sometimes translated as gentleness, moderation, gentle spirit, temperance, patience, forbearance, modesty, mildness, and reasonableness! Wow! What a range of meaning! The idea is embodied in a sweet reasonableness. It is not insisting on the letter of the law. Two examples of this kind of thinking are of St. Joseph's decision to divorce Mary quietly, rather than expose her to harsher punishments, until the angel informs Joseph that Mary conceived of the Holy Spirit. What faith! What forbearance! What gentleness! The second example is the woman caught in adultery (John 8:1-11). We all know how Jesus wrote in the sand, how he said "let anyone among you who is without sin be the first to throw a stone at her" (John 8:7b). This is the kind of thing that should accompany our Christian walk. And we don't walk just Willy-nilly; we will soon see that our walk is situated on a royal road.

Paul is giving this advice while he is held prisoner at Rome. While waiting for what was potentially a death penalty, Paul is telling the Philippians to rejoice, not once but twice. Before leaving the topic of gentleness, let's have a look at a few more clues about this quality that should inform our joy in the Lord. The word "gentleness" is sometimes used to translate the Hebrew word *hesed,* which is often translated as **loving-kindness**. Here we begin to understand the word, which is so difficult to translate adequately, "gentleness." Loving-kindness is the customary, enduring attitude of God. I believe it is this aspect of God's perfection that we Christians are told to copy: "Be perfect, therefore, as your heavenly Father is **perfect**"[11] (Matthew 5:48).

Are there clues here as to why we Christians don't show forth more joy? We will examine these in detail later. For now, we consider the most general outlines. Perhaps one reason we hang on to our long faces is that we don't recognize that the "Lord is near." The word translated as "near" does not tell if it means the Lord is close physically or in time. Suffice it to say the form of the proximity is less important than the fact of the Lord's closeness.

Perhaps what all this about is seeing things with God's eyes. Many years ago, while attending Mass in our parish chapel, the preacher presented an interactive reflection about the posture and positions of prayer. The priest would demonstrate the different uses of the hands in prayer. He began with hands joined, fingers intertwined. Each member of the congregation was called upon to comment on it. One person said it seems devotional. Another said, "I feel alone." At the far end of the chapel was a Japanese man, who said, "God is strong."

The priest then held up folded hands in the traditional prayer style. Opinions of the gathered worshippers ranged from "old-fashioned" to "rigid." The Japanese visitor said, "God is holy!" When he said this I felt peace, which was also humbling.

Clearly, we were all thinking about the prayer on our own terms. Now the priest raised holy hands, raising them above his head in supplication. The rest of us expressed how "modern and current" it felt; how "liberated," The Japanese man, with great recollection, offered, "God is merciful!" It was the first and only time we ever saw that holy man; or was he an angel? The point is that he thought of everything in terms of God, not just one's own feelings; he appeared to be seeking God. How wonderful if we could realize that the Lord is near in the way the Japanese man did that day.

I'm sure we must all have moments in our lives when we felt the particular nearness of Christ. This is an ingredient in our joy. It is seeing ourselves, at least at times, as God sees us. Over a decade ago I was in the hospital suffering from an overdose of aspirin. The hallucinations were horrendous. At one point in my delusions, I came before the throne of grace. I heard a Voice say, "What do you have to show me?"

There was a great white throne, so high you could not see who sat upon it. I interpreted the question as an invitation for me so tell the Voice my good deeds. In front of me was a long black table such as one finds in court. I said that I had worked with others to provide showers, clothing, and job training for the homeless. As a token I placed something that look like a hockey puck on the table. But the voice said, "You got a lot of positive publicity and respect from civic leaders. You've had your reward!"

Next, I said that over the years I had helped to save many marriages through counseling. But the Voice said, "Many of those couples were so happy, paid you back in gifts and praise. You've had your reward!" I placed another black disk on the table. I continued to suggest good deeds and the Voice continued to minimize them. Pretty soon the table was covered with the tokens. I began to conclude that after all the sacrifices and suffering in my life, I was going to hell! What a feeling of desolation! I pray you will never experience that feeling no matter how fleeting. Then the Voice said, "You must see yourself as I see you." My imagination went wild with panic! Then the Voice said, "You must see yourself as I see you; you are my beloved son." It turned out that even in this dark moment God was near. Perhaps if we recall those moments when God has been near us, we will be just that much closer to releasing the Christian joy that will draw others to the Savior!

Another reason that may keep us from full attainment of joy in the Lord is **worry**. In *Philippians* 4:6, Paul tells us not to worry. The word translated as "worry" is *merimáo*. This is perhaps more than any other the thief of joy. We will discuss this in greater detail later. For now, we need to keep in mind that the word "worry" means to be drawn in different directions.

This leads us to discuss the role of prayer in the acquisition of joy in Christ. A great part of our Christian joy is directly related to prayer. Here we are called to thanksgiving and petition. John Chrysostom (349–407) reminds us that to pray and give thanks in all things means that God wants not only our requests, but also our praise—that is, our thanks. "So one ought to give thanks for everything, even what seems grievous. That is the mark of one who is truly thankful."[12] This prayer leads to the "Peace, which surpasses all understanding" (Phil. 4:7a). Such peace is the diadem that crowns our joy! This is the peace that reconciles all things in heaven and on earth (Col. 1:20). This peace will guard our hearts. The peace of the Lord is posted as a lookout for our safety, the sentry of our joy and the promises of Christ. This passage should help us along the way on knowing and expressing joy in our lives. This passage can give us peace in unsettling times.

CHAPTER FOUR

KILL JOYS

During my first year in seminary, my class went on an offsite retreat. It had been one of the stormiest winters we experienced in Northern California. There was heavy rain and savage winds. One of our first events was a faith walk. We met in the gym. There were two stages at either end of the cavernous room. We gathered at one of the stages. On the apron of that stage were many lighted candles. We were supposed to pick up one of the candles and walk step by step toward the opposite stage. Each step we were supposed to recall a blessing or a kindness that God has shown us. The side doors to the gym were left open, creating a cross draft. I had determined to give thanks for a different memory of my wife, Lori. The others appeared to be making good progress, but I had barely begun to move. The wind was blowing. I was afraid that my candle would go out. I was experiencing anxiety. Would my candle go out? Would I be embarrassed in front of my classmates? Would I be able to concentrate on the blessings of my wonderful wife?

Then I looked down at my hands that were cupping the candle. I was so protective of the flame that I could barely walk. I suddenly realized that I had been walking that way most of my life. I thought to myself that anxiety had kept me from boldly stepping out. My heart was not under the watch of that grace that leads to peace beyond all understanding.

You see our joy, our faith, and our very living of the Christian life is guarded like a sentry. But what exactly is guarded? In other words, what are those things that can subdue or even seem to kill our joy in the Lord? A faith walk is a great way to count blessings. In a family setting, sharing stories about our blessings can be very supportive and inspiring for us and/or our children. There are many invaders trying to steal our joy. Among these are false humility, anxiety, worldly concerns, and spiritual legalism.

False humility, false pride, and unconfessed sins are spiritual combatants attacking us in order to steal our joy. These are largely based on aberrations of who we are. Being humble before the Lord—in short, true humility—does not mean we act as wimps. True humility doesn't present itself as negating one's own talent. Sometimes the way to acknowledge compliments is merely to say "Thank you." I once knew a truly gifted pianist. He had a touch you could recognize without seeing who was playing. Yet when he was complimented, he would sometimes argue with one paying tribute—essentially denying his skill, his God-given skill. This is an example of false humility.

It seems that one of the main remedies to everything standing in the way of experiencing and expressing joy is an incorrect perception of our true worth. This has something to do with what the Voice said to me, "You must see yourself as I see you; you are my beloved child." True humility before God is so necessary not only for the release of joy, but also for living the Christian life. This is the case because it was the attitude of our Lord and Savior. Once again we look to the *Letter to the Philippians:*

> Let the same mind be in you that was in Christ Jesus, who though he was in the form of God did not regard equality with God as something to be exploited, but emptied himself, taking the form of a slave, being born in human likeness. And being found in human form, he humbled himself and became obedient to the point of death— even death on a cross (Phil. 2:6-8).

So, first Paul exhorts us to have the same mind that was in Christ Jesus. This means to think of things in the same way Jesus thinks of things. Clearly this passage reflects on Jesus' knowledge that he had equality with God, which was true; the humility came in his not using this knowledge, allowing him to sacrifice his life on the cross. Real humility begins with the realization we are God's children, made in his **image** and **likeness.** This should not puff us up, but help us to pour ourselves out for others.

The point here is that false humility and/or pride can be a bar to experiencing and expressing joy. But the Lord has provided some remedies to release the joy that is an essential part of the Christian walk. For many of us, God initiates the change that leads to joy and the fulfilling Christian life that accompanies it. No less than Saint Peter himself has provided us a remedy to change from an unfeeling, plodding Christian life to a vibrant, feeling, and dynamic adventure in God's grace. It begins with: "Humble yourself under the mighty hand of God so that he may exalt you in due time (I Pet. 5:6). In this passage it appears that we are supposed to be the one doing the humbling. Sometimes this is true. But the passage also means that we need to allow ourselves to become lowly, to realize that God is God and we are not. We must remember that our current quest is overcoming anxiety, because anxiety steals our joy. We need to remember also that our humility is designed only to raise us up. He humbles us to exalt us. That is, he will show us our true lowliness so that he can raise us up to true humility!

But what should we do with our **anxiety**? How can we deal with this great block to our joy? Peter tells us to "Cast all your anxiety on him because he cares for you (I Pet. 5:7). God is telling us trust him enough to take our anxieties and toss them on to the Lord. What's more, He invites, even commands us to toss our cares and distractions on to him because we matter to him! St. John the Baptist says, "Here is the Lamb of God who takes away the sin of the world" (John 1:29). If he takes away our sins, how much more will he take away our false humility and false pride!

Step one is being humbled so that God can exalt us. Step two is to consciously toss our cares and anxieties on the Lord. Step three is to "Discipline yourselves; keep alert. Like a roaring lion your adversary the devil prowls around, looking for some to devour" (I Pet. 5:8). The Greek text uses the word *nepho* for "dicipline yourselves," or "be sober." Essentially this means to abstain from drunkedness. We are told to stay on guard so that the Evil One may not pounce on us and have us for lunch. Thus, step four is to guard and protect yourselves against becoming the prey of the devil. This is one way we can hold on to our joy in the Lord.

We find another remedy for joylessness in *Ephesians* chapter five. This one builds on the passage form *First Peter*:

> Do not get drunk with wine, for that is debauchery; but be filled with The Spirit, as you sing **psalms** and **hymns** and spiritual **songs** among yourselves, singing and making melody to the Lord in your hearts, giving thanks to God the Father at all times and for everything in the name of our Lord Jesus Christ (Eph. 5:18-20).

This remedy opens a very important inducement to joy. First, we must keep in mind the vital importance of being filled with the Spirit. This is so important that we will devote an entire chapter to it. For now, we will take up the importance of music as a way of drawing us in to Joy and as a remedy for indifference and coldness in our faith.

Being filled with the Spirit bids us to sing and the song feeds our joy. Very specifically, we are to sing psalms. This means not only should we sing actual biblical psalms, but also music in the style of the book of *Psalms;* that is to say song with a string accompaniment.

In an important passage of First Corinthians, St. Paul talks about the charismatic gifts, but makes a remarkable statement about prayer and singing: "I will pray with the spirit, but I will pray with the mind also; I will sing praise with the spirit, but I will sing praise with the mind also" (I Cor. 14:15). Again, we will turn to this in greater depth later on. For now, suffice it to say that the Lord encourages us to sing in tongues and to sing in psalms and hymns and spiritual songs! These lead from praise to joy. They also facilitate joy!

We find another remedy to heavy-heartedness in the book of *Proverbs*. We must remember that one of the primary downers in the Christian life is anxiety. "Anxiety weighs down the human heart, but a good word cheers it up" (Prov. 12:25). So here is a third remedy for our lack of joy: fellowship. This is why the Church is not a solitary affair. It is particularly difficult when people are confined to their homes. It is one reason why assembly is required. That is why the motivation of the whole charismatic renewal is the building up of the Body of Christ. It is not a religion of private, you-and-me-Jesus, but rather a living body. Jesus sent out the 72 in pairs. God is a community of persons. Faith in Christ is above all about relationship, belonging.

So it is important that we have goodly fellowship. This tendency of rugged individualism in the faith is not the way of Christ. Even those called to a contemplative life are not truly solitary. Most contemplatives live in community. Being separated from others is **not** the teaching of Jesus. Yet many Christians live as if the faith was just "me and Jesus." Many years ago I read an article in the Catholic press, which is emblematic of this breach of the faith that leads to a lack of joy and peace in our lives. The article was lamenting the anonymous Christianity with which many of us are familiar. It lamented that we go to Communion as strangers, and we return to our pews as strangers. Thank God that much of this is changing today as we tune in to the message of the Lord, rather than focusing on the mechanics. Order is needed in worship, to be sure—even in the prayer meeting. St. Paul devotes entire chapters to this topic, yet it is words and actions of worship that constitute the heart of our faith. One caveat about fellowship: We must avoid comparison. President Theodore Roosevelt said, "Comparison is the thief of joy."[13] We must not compare our gifts with those of others. St. Paul tells us, "We do not dare to classify or compare ourselves with some of those who commend themselves. But when they measure themselves by one another, and compare themselves with one another, they do not show good sense. (2 Cor. 10:12).

There are two further considerations in light of the cultivation and protection of joy. The first is legalism. We are saved by grace, not by law. This grace was imparted through the merits of Christ on the cross. It is not our keeping the commandments that brings us salvation. It is also not choosing Jesus as Lord and Savior. The Lord himself tells us, "You did not choose me but I chose you. And I appointed that you go and bear fruit, fruit that will last, so that the Father will give you whatever you ask in my name" (John 15:16). Legalism would substitute salvation by works rather than grace. If I keep myself as a staunch law-keeper and suppose that act alone will bring salvation, it seems as if I bypass the outpouring of God's grace. It is through faith in him that we are saved. Yet it is by our deeds that we will be judged. We have nothing more to do to illustrate this point than to read Matthew 25:31-46. Also, let us add another passage from *Second*

Corinthians: "For all of us must appear before the judgment seat of Christ, so that each may receive recompense for what they have done in the body, whether good or evil" (II Cor. 5:10). While we are saved by grace, we are judged by our actions. Legalism jumps to the conclusion that it all depends on our works. Quite frequently legalism can drag us further into comparison and judgment. Its stance is, if I can keep all these commands, and you don't seem to be able to, then I'm a better Christian than you are. It helps to produce a culture of checklists of sanctity, a sanctity that masquerades as judgment in place of love, hard-heartedness in place of love, and self-righteousness in place of joy!

Another related, but less seemingly religious equivalent is the "I did it my way" version of the Christian faith. It may give us a temporary moment of "happiness"—that is, the notion that everything is going well because it is my solitary standard that determines what my walk with Christ is. The call to the Christian faith is the call to holiness. To be holy is to be set apart for God. God calls us to holiness and then equips us to serve him, not to be served. God's grace allows us to cooperate with his grace.

Sin is an obstacle to joy in our lives, especially sins that have not been confessed. True sorrow for sin can rightly keep true peace away from us. Sometimes we don't confess certain sins because we think somehow God is angry with us. This was illustrated one year for our school's Reconciliation service. It was in the middle of the Winter Olympics. The night before a woman skater had fallen on her backside during her program. I held up a silver ice skate and asked the students if any of them knew much about ice-skating.

I told the young people of the sacrifices her parents had undoubtedly undergone to help to get her to the Olympics. "What do you think?" I asked them. "Were her parents angry with her?"

The answers of the children were pretty uniform. They said the parents would embrace their child and tell her they loved her. I them told them it is just like that whenever we sin. We should never try to hide or ignore our sins; God is predisposed to save us.

One of the signs that we are growing in this task is the presence of joy. It is difficult to over-estimate the importance of joy in our lives. Grace, which leads to joy, is fed by a proper assessment of ourselves as regards humility. Grace that leads to joy calls us to humility. Song leads to joy. True worship leads to joy. We should encounter this joy in the Prayer Meeting, the study of the Bible, and the Eucharistic assembly, where we are made present at the saving sacrifice of the cross.

CHAPTER FIVE

JOY AND HAPPINESS

We continue to ask, what is joy? How is it different from happiness? How can I keep it in good times and in bad? And above all, how can I find it?

Joy is defined as a feeling of great pleasure and happiness. We have already learned that Christian joy is a celebration of reality of our Lord that God has broken into history. Joy is also based in the deliverance given by the Lord over slavery to sin and death as witnessed by the Passover and the Resurrection from the tomb of our Savior, Jesus Christ. So the first distinction we need to make is between a worldly definition of joy and the joy that leads to peace surpassing all understanding. Let's examine some of the writings of the Fathers of the Church and great theologians.

Some thoughts about the heart of the Church from the mind of the Church:

> Joy destroys sadness, in tragedy it gives patience,
> in prayers it gives grace, in labors and struggles

it gives delight, in obedience it gives merriment, in hospitality it gives shelter, in hope it gives recourse, in mourning it gives comfort, in sorrow it gives assistance, in love it gives decoration, and in patience it gives reward.[14] (Abbas Nilus +430)

For this Orthodox saint, joy is so much more than a pleasant emotion. He is supported in this by many other Fathers and theologians. St. Thomas wrote extensively about Christian joy. The Dominican saint distinguishes two reasons for Christian joy. These are joy in the Divine goodness in itself and our joy in participating in the divine goodness.[15] Accordingly, there is a part of Christian joy that cannot change; it is based on God in himself. There is a part that might be variable because it is based on our participation in the joy of the Lord. In our own time, Peter Kreeft, the great Thomistic scholar, refers to a modern world-view concerning happiness and joy. Kreeft alludes to the Freudian notion that "joy" is a substitute for physical pleasure. Kreeft characterizes Freud as saying that people become saints out of sexual frustrations.[16] "Joy is more than happiness, just as happiness is more than pleasure. Pleasure is in the body. Happiness is in the mind and feelings. Joy is deep in the heart, the spirit, the center of the self."[17]

This might explain how it is possible to experience joy even in the midst of trials, persecution and illness. The foundation of joy in the Lord is in the Lord himself. The Lord doesn't change. This is the chief difference between joy and happiness. The basis of Christian joy doesn't change. Our circumstances do change. If

Christian joy were determined by what is going on, it is not joy, but happiness.

There is a true happiness. It is like false happiness dependent on circumstances. True happiness is accepting a legitimate pleasure or good fortune that is not contrary to the call and command of God. The Christian needs to understand that embracing the good gifts of God is temporary in this life. In other words, we need to rightly divide our life circumstances. Happiness is temporary; joy in the Lord is permanent.

What the world offers instead of joy is entertainment. We make entertainment of everything. Justice becomes entertainment. Look at the number of judge shows on television. Crime is presented as entertainment. Adultery and perversion—even the notion that there is such a thing as perversion is presented as entertainment. "Doing wrong is like sport to a fool, but wise conduct is pleasure to a person of understanding" (Proverbs 10:23). Other versions translate this passage as, "Crime is the entertainment of the fool" (Rheims-Douay Version). When we adopt worldly entertainment as our delight, we expose ourselves to valuing what the forces opposed to God believe. Peggy Lee's hit song from the late sixties, "Is That All There Is?"[18] bespeaks the results of trying to substitute "happiness" for "joy." The lyrics seem to be in despair over seeing life as a great letdown, a let-down so strong as to lead only to drinking and living a life in pursuit of pleasure. The sentiments expressed in the above song encapsulate much of the philosophy that underpins modern pessimism. The classical expression of religion and reason is embodied in the writings of St. Anselm of Canterbury 1033–1109). The relationship between faith and reason is revealed in Plato and Aristotle. In our own age, Francis Shaeffer (1912–1984), the noted Protestant theologian, correctly points to what he calls the line of dispair. Shaeffer holds that Kierkegaard's "leap of faith" led to the divorce of faith from reason. There is therefore no truth and no non-truth in antithesis, no right or wrong—you are adrift.[19] To this we add excessive individualism. Think of Sinatra's "My Way."[20] The Bible tells us, "Sometimes there is a way that seems to be right, but in the end it is the way to death" (Prov. 16:25). These two trends, despair and the supremacy of the individual as the ultimate moral authority, are changing the landscape of freedom and responsibility. So today people are fired because they point out that there are only two sexes—no matter that there are only xy and xx chromosomes. This all leads to further despair. If we listen to the propaganda of the pit, we will gravitate toward what they call happiness, which can be defined as loveless sex or drug abuse; we will not experience the true joy of the Lord. Such are the ramifications of choosing happiness rather than joy.

But wait. There's more! Joy is not somehow disconnected from our Christian walk. Joy does not separate faith from reason. Joy, as we have seen, endures. And there is a reason for this.

It is revealed in the source of the words for joy and grace. Surprise: They have the same root. Let us seen how that reality operates.

Three words that don't necessarily seem directly related are important to our quest for joy. These words are: joy, **grace,** and **gifts**. In some ways, even in English, we can easily see some relationship between them. But there is a theological and practical connection between these words. To show this we must look at these words in Greek. They all begin with the same letter, "X" (pronounced "Chi" or "Kai"): Chará, Cháris, and Charísmata: Joy, grace, and gifts, respectively. First, the word we know began as a greeting. As such it appears in the word of the Angel Gabriel to the Blessed Virgin. In fact, this passage (Luke 1:28) is a great opportunity to learn something about these words. First, the angel greets Mary, "Χαιρε." This is usually translated as "hail." But it certainly has greater meaning than that. It was used as a standard greeting in letters in the time of the Roman Empire. In the Pauline epistles the word is often translated as "grace"; for example "Grace to you and peace from God our Father and the Lord Jesus Christ" (Romans 1:7b). Now back to the Annunciation. The word following the greeting is also a form of χάρις. It is often translated as "full of grace." It can also mean "highly favored" or "highly favored one."

So joy differs from happiness in that joy in the Lord is permanent while happiness is temporary. Joy leads to fulfillment, while happiness can lead to despair, especially as a result of disconnection between faith and reason, form and function, and observation and reality.

CHAPTER SIX

BAPTISM IN THE HOLY SPIRIT

On the Great Vigil of Easter the first year of my first pastor-ate, we had the most wonderful walk-in font; it was designed for full immersion. The water was about five feet high. When I entered it, the only part of me you could see was my head. Add to that the fact that the walls of the font were about three to four feet higher—about eight feet altogether. The effect was that I completely disappeared from the sight of the congregation! The Assembly went wild with laughter. Although this was among the most solemn rites of the Easter Vigil, I felt I couldn't let them have the last word. Going up a step or two and raising myself to my full height, I waved at the people above the wall of the font! While the action wasn't exactly loaded with formality, the laugh-ter led to a warmer reception for the several being baptized that night. Joy entered to make that Vigil a night of delight as well as of great solemnity. Joy has a way of doing that!

Yet our pursuit of joy is not an end in itself. It is a result of faith in Christ Jesus. It is not derived from an incident or slip of the lip. The presence of joy is not our doing, but the product of the Holy Spirit. In fact, one the events that got me thinking about the importance of joy in the Lord happened years before that when my cousin Rudy, who was a permanent deacon, was preaching. His homily was on Luke 8, which is essentially, a description of those who accompanied Jesus early in his ministry. He said, "…and Mary Magdalene, from who he cast out seven deacons." He quickly corrected his words to say "seven demons." Needless to say there was a smile on everyone's face. In that moment, it occurred to me that we seem to be joyful in church only when someone makes some form of mistake. This seemed to be a mistake in itself. Shouldn't we experience a joyful, positive encounter with the Lord? Christian joy is not based on the incongruity or malapropisms.

Baptism not only produces joy, but is also a spiritual life empowered by faith. It is a Bible-believing, miracle-believing, magisterium-believing, overcoming faith. For the Christian, life begins at Baptism. The Bible and tradition teach us that Baptism has several effects. What is this bath of grace? First, it is clear from the sacred scriptures that Baptism is necessary for salvation. Jesus tells us, "Very truly, I tell you, no one can enter the kingdom of God without being born of water and Spirit" (John. 3:5).[21]

This is how one enters into the life of faith. St. Peter preached the necessity of Baptism in his Pentecost sermon. The people heard him speak of how the people rejected the true Messiah of Israel and crucified him. They were cut to the heart, and asked, "What must we do?" St. Peter responded, "Repent and be baptized every one of you in the name of Jesus Christ so that your sins may be forgiven and you will receive the gift of the Holy Spirit" (Acts 2:38).[22] It is likely that being baptized in the name of Jesus was to distinguish it from the baptism of John, or pagan baptisms such as that of Mithraism. Water baptism applies to John's Baptism; it was for repentance only. Baptism of the Savior is in the name of the Holy Trinity; it is Baptism by water and the Spirit. And it not only includes repentance, but also forgiveness of sins! The sacrament conforms us to Christ as prophet, priest, and king; Baptism makes us children of the living God. So it is not correct to speak of Christian sacramental Baptism as "water baptism." Water is, of course, the matter of the sacrament. Yet, the sacrament also gives grace and the seeds of the Holy Spirit. Likewise, the sacrament of Confirmation also confers the Holy Spirit. It is important to remember that Baptism and Confirmation were once a single rite. Both confer the graces needed for Christian living, but often we go through life without opening those gifts—without releasing the power of these sacraments.

So then, what is Baptism in the Holy Spirit? First, Sacramental Baptism imparts the Holy Spirit. But what may be called Baptism in the Holy Spirit or the "release of the Holy Spirit" is necessary for triumphant, joyful Christian living.

Therefore, we see that Baptism in the Holy Spirit is not a sacrament in the sense that it is an outward sign instituted by Christ to give grace. Release of the Spirit indeed gives grace— very special grace; these gifts are intended for people who are pursuing the Christian life of grace, those who know the Lord Jesus and desire to make him known to others. St. Paul informs us that these gifts differ from one another. They are given for the sake of the building up of the Body of Christ.

We see that Baptism in the Holy Spirit is not a sacrament as one of the seven sacraments, but acts as the catalyst that unleashes the charismatic gifts and leads to a profusion of the fruit of the Spirit. This is a secret to many Christians, but in times of alienation and separation such as we now face, it is essential. How should we understand Baptism in the Holy Spirit? Cardinal Suenens (1904–1996) commented: "To interpret the Renewal as a 'movement' among other movements is to misunderstand its nature; it is a movement of the Spirit offered to the entire Church and destined to rejuvenate every part of the Church's life."[23] But were these charismatic gifts only operative in the apostolic church? Are they essentially a modern invention? If these gifts are ancient and continuing, why did they decline?

This leads us to briefly discuss three different views of Baptism in the Holy Spirit. The earliest and most pervasive interpretation of the Baptism in the Holy Spirit is stirring up, releasing, or actualizing the grace and presence of the Holy Spirit already conferred in Baptism and Confirmation. In this theory, the release of the Holy Spirit and the charismatic gifts are normative for the Christian. Killian McDonnel and George T. Montague provide an impressive inventory of early Church Fathers.[24] St. Hilary of Poitier (315–367) describes the experience of Baptism: "We who have been reborn through the sacrament of baptism experience intense joy (*maximum gaudium*) when we feel within us the first stirring of the Holy Spirit."[25] A large cloud of witnesses testify to the public and liturgical nature of Baptism in the Holy Spirit; for many of the Church Fathers, this baptism is synonymous with Christian initiation.

I present this information for a number of reasons. If you have been baptized, but have not received the charisms (gifts) of the Holy Spirit, I hope to show you that these gifts are normative and necessary for the Church. I also hope to stir up in you the desire for these gifts. They are grounded not only in the sacred scriptures but also in the early practice of the Church.

St. Cyril of Jerusalem (313–386) wrote at length about the Sacrament of Baptism. He called the Spirit a new kind of water. "The Spirit sanctifies the Christian, transforming the baptized into the likeness of Christ."[26] St. Cyril goes on to pray: "God grant that you may be worthy of the charisms of prophecy."[27]

The skeptic might say, I never heard of this. I don't remember hearing this in Catechism. Isn't this something totally new? Not according to the record of the *Acts of the Apostles,* and the first three-hundred years of Christianity. So what happened? St. John Chrysostom (349–407) expresses a sorrow over the decline of the charismatic gifts: "Whoever was baptized at once spoke in tongues, and not only in tongues, but many prophesied; some performed many other wonderful works."[28]

Before leaving the first interpretation of Baptism in the Holy Spirit we must look at the premise that Baptism partook of the sacramental teaching that Baptism forgives all sins, incorporates the person into the Body of Christ, and conforms the baptized into the image of Christ, Prophet, Priest, and King. It also imparts the Holy Spirit. If the interpretation is correct— that is, if the charismatic gifts were traditionally imparted in the first centuries—why do we not experience them as a rule today? So what happened?

There seem to be several reasons for the decline in the manifestation of the Charismatic Gifts.[29] One reason for the decline in imparting the charisms was the success of Christianity. There was great increase of the Christian faith in the Roman Empire. Paganism became less practiced, especially after the Edict of Milan (313). This document made Christianity legal in the Roman Empire. The church began to grow. After a time, with the decline of instructions and mass "conversions," people were baptized because the ruler of the region encouraged his subjects to be baptized. Early in the history of the Church, a heresy called Montanism began to replace the revealed truth of the Gospel with "prophecy" from the cult of Montanus (fl.150). This cult taught that private prophecy replaced and often contradicted the Holy Bible. This made large segments of the Church shy away from what had been a mainstay of Baptism, the gift of tongues, prophecy, and the other Charismatic Gifts. To repeat, this first way of looking at the Baptism of the Holy Spirit sees it as normative for all Christians.

A second way of looking at Baptism in the Holy Spirit is viewing it as a special outpouring to equip the believer for some specific mission. This theory might best align with the notion of special grace. The gifts of the Holy Spirit, especially those we call charismatic gifts, are not limited directly and exclusively by sacraments:

There are furthermore *special graces,* also called *charisms* after the Greek term used by St. Paul and meaning "favor," "gratuitous gift," "benefit." Whatever their character—sometimes it is extraordinary, such as the gift of miracles or of tongues, or prophecy—charisms are oriented toward sanctifying grace and are intended for the common good of the Church. They are at the service of charity, which builds up the Church (Catechism of the Catholic Church, 2003).

The Church also recognizes something called graces of state. These are gifts of the Spirit summarized in *The Letter to the Romans:* "We have gifts that differ according to the grace given to us: prophecy in proportion to faith; ministry, in ministering; the teacher, in teaching; the exhorter in exhortation; the giver, in generosity; the leader in diligence; the compassionate, in cheerfulness" (Rom. 12:6-8). This passage is quoted in the *Catechism of the Catholic Church (2004).* We know that grace is given not only in and by sacraments, but also by many other means. It is rather like the situation in *Acts of the Apostles,* chapter 4 (Acts 3-4:31), where the disciples pray for **boldness** after being instructed by the Sanhedrin to no longer preach or heal in the name of Jesus. "When they prayed, the place in which they were gathered together was shaken; and they were filled with the Holy Spirit and spoke the word of God with boldness" (Acts 4:31). Notice that the general charismatic Gifts are not mentioned here, but only the boldness for which they prayed. This means that this particular outpouring of the Spirit doesn't appear to be normative for the whole Church, nor does it appear to be related to Christian Initiation.

A third theory of Baptism in the Holy Spirit views the gifts as functioning in a world approaching the second coming of Christ. It, like the second theory, views the imparting of the Spirit as occasional and for specific purposes. In this case, the gifts are offered for the preaching of the second coming of Christ. We must remember that the early Church seemed to live in the almost immediate expectation of the glorious return of the Lord. This third theory sees the Charismatic Gifts as tools for the final evangelism before the Lord's return. This is emphasized in time of distress and anxiety.

There are a few things we must take into consideration. We must remember that theories are developed to attempt to explain events. It seems to me that the first of these approaches best explains the presence of the Charismatic Gifts as they appear in the New Testament, the preponderance of references to the Gifts by a large number of Church Fathers. Above all, the first theory is connected with full Christian Initiation. That being said, there is no reason why all three cannot be true. Yet, the most effective, universal, and normative interpretation is that the imparting of the Gifts accompanies and completes Christian initiation! We must pray for and expect the Baptism in the Holy Spirit.

Given the ancient nature of the Baptism of the Holy Spirit and acknowledging the importance of how the Gifts equip the Christian for victorious living, we must ask the question: How can I receive the Baptism of the Holy Spirit? How can the Holy Spirit be released in my life? Luke comments on earthly fathers as they give good things to their children. Jesus asks, "If you then, who are evil, know how to give good gifts to your children, how much more will your heavenly Father give the Holy Spirit to those who ask him" (Lk.11:13). So what is a Life in the Spirit seminar? In June, Pope Francis addressed a worldwide retreat for clergy. Addressing a gathering at Saint John Lateran Church in Rome, the Pontiff addressed them as dispensers of grace. "Speaking of dispensers of grace, I ask each and all of you that as part of the current of grace of Charismatic Renewal you organize seminars of Life in the Spirit in your parishes and seminaries, schools, in neighborhoods, to share Baptism in the Spirit," said Francis. "It is catechesis. It is catechesis that produces, by the work of the Holy Spirit, the personal encounter with Jesus who changes our life."[30]

How do we ask for the Baptism in the Holy Spirit? What steps might we follow? First, we need to confess our sins. Especially important in this inventory are sins dealing with the occult. Some of these might seem trifling like using Ouija boards, horoscopes, or even watching movies with satanic themes. One can catch evil. In fact, like many other things, we catch them rather than learn them. So let us confess any kind of proximity we have had with the occult. In *Acts,* the giving up of occult activity is very important.

> A number of those who practiced magic collected
> their books And burned them publicly; when the
> value of these books was calculated, it was found
> to come to fifty thousand silver coins. So the

word of the Lord grew mightily and prevailed. (Acts 19:19-20).

Second, we must ask for the Gifts of the Holy Spirit. Remember, "Ask, and it will be given to you; search, and you will find; knock, and the door will be opened for you. For everyone who asks receives, and everyone who searches finds, and for everyone who, knocks, the door will be opened" (Matthew 7:7-8). Lest we say, "I knocked, and nothing happened." We cannot say, "been there done that." Let's keep in mind an interesting feature of Greek grammar: the durative quality of present-tense verbs. We ought to hear the Lord telling us to "keep asking, keep knocking and keep searching." Morale: If you ask the Lord for the Gift of the Holy Spirit and don't receive it rapidly, remember to keep asking the Lord.

How might we do that? The easiest way is tell the Lord "I want everything, every gift you have for me!" The beauty of this request is that God already desires us to have the fullness of his gifts that we might in turn build up his Body. One often receives baptism in the Holy Spirit in the setting of a special teaching about the gifts and the fullness of the empowered Christian. One of the usual ways people are introduced to these wonderful gifts is through a Life in the Spirit Seminar. If you have not yet received this second blessing, watch your church bulletin, or diocesan newspaper, or contact your charismatic renewal office. Seminars may be over several weeks or on occasion, may be done over a weekend or on a Saturday.

Before moving on, let me clarify the difference between praying in a tongue, and the gift of tongues. Praying in tongues is for the personal expression of the love of God in the life of individual Christians. "For we do not know how to pray as we ought, but that very Spirit intercedes with sighs too deep for words" (Rom. 8:26b). Praying in tongues is mainly for the edification of the individual. Speaking in tongues is the proclamation of a message from God in a language unknown to the one who speaks it, but interpreted by someone else in the prayer meeting.

In my first assignment as a priest, I attended a charismatic prayer meeting at St. Leander's church in San Leandro. A woman stood up and began to speak in a foreign language. When she had finished, another woman rose to translate. The original language was Swahili (the proclaimer did not know a single word in that language). The interpreter was a native speaker of Swahili who was visiting from Africa. The Lord's message of praise was proclaimed—signs and wonders. A little later, another person began to speak in a language they didn't know. While my Greek isn't perfect, I could understand and interpret much of what that sister was saying. This kind of tongues is there for the unity of people from different cultures and language groups, to praise God and to build up the Body of Christ. Many people will never directly experience the Charismatic gift of tongues, but I believe that God wishes to impart a personal prayer language to all. The actual meaning of the language we may use in prayer is unimportant because of its purpose. St. Paul explains, "For if I pray in a tongue, my spirit prays but my mind is unproductive. What should I do then? I will pray with the Spirit, but I will pray with the mind also" (I Cor.14:14-15b). The prayer language builds up the individual; the proclamation of message in a tongue needs to be interpreted and is there to edify the whole Body.

CHAPTER SEVEN

The Royal Road to Joy

The primary focus of this book is living a life of Christian joy. You might ask, "Why are you spending so much time on Baptism of the Holy Spirit and the charismatic gifts?" The answer is that we are seeking joy that is spiritual, a joy that is deeper than circumstances, and a joy that the sorrows and challenges of this world cannot rob from us. Therefore, our joy must be grounded in the Spirit and hence the emphasis on the gifts of the Spirit.

This road, this way, is not frequented—but it is a royal road. One characteristic of a royal road is rapid communications across distances. The model for the metaphor was the construction of the Royal Road, a famous road. It was route from Susa in Persia, modern Iran to Sardis in Asia Minor, modern Turkey. It was an ancient highway, rebuilt by Darius the Great in the fifth century B.C. This road was about 1,677 miles long. It took nine days to traverse the route, whereas other routes could take up to ninety days. Royal decrees and official government business predominated the traffic along this way.

The New Testament biblical word for "**way**" is the word for "road." Jesus says to us, "I am the way, the truth and the life" (John 14:6). One of the first mentions of this road of the Lord is in the prophet Isaiah. "A voice cries out: 'In the wilderness prepare the way of the Lord, make straight in the desert a highway for our God'" (Isa. 40:3). The royal road of the Lord is again referenced when the Blessed Virgin goes to the hill country of Judea to visit her kinswoman, Elizabeth. The father of John the Baptist recognizes that the Lord will guide our feet into the *way* of peace (Lk. 1:72). We encounter this royal road again in the prophet Malachi: "See, I am sending my messenger to prepare the way before me" (Malachi 3:1). This same passage goes on to tell us that the Lord will enter his temple. This royal road, this kingly way was to become the way of the cross. We must also remember that the earliest name for Christians was "people of the way."

Before proceeding, we must look at how language morphs. The word "way," both in Hebrew and in Greek, originally signifies a road, royal or otherwise. Because a road led from one place to another, the word began to take on an even-wider meaning, the journey and the means of arriving at your destination. The word also came to mean a method for doing something.

Coming to the Lord on the royal road has numerous advantages. It is direct. It is directed toward God, not our own will. Progressing on this road constitutes real freedom. It is a virtual spiritual journey that can take us from walking in the bad news and worse conditions. We find ourselves coming to the Lord without the list of "gimmies." Lord, gimme this or that. Lord, help my daughter, but in the way *I* want her to be helped. This attitude invades my prayers and intercessions before the throne of grace. In other words, when we approach the Lord on the royal road, we come to him, allowing him to be fully sovereign, and allowing ourselves to be fully his child.

Prayer along the royal road looks and feels different. Our eyes are directed to outcomes that are not seated in our own will, but in God's will. Prayer along the way is not in the emotions. We can bring emotion to our prayers, but we can receive from God without expectations—except that God will act in God's way and in God's time. This can help to remove one of the most insidious elements of modern living. Mental and physical stress is said to cause $300 billion each year according to a study by the American Psychological Association.[31]

As King's kids we have the right to use the royal road! Further there are distinct disadvantages for progressing by other means. The contrast here is between the self-serving lyrics to the Sinatra hit, *My Way,* and entering the sanctuary "…by the new and living way that Jesus opened for us through the curtain (that is his flesh)" (See Heb. 10:19-21). The passage from Hebrews indicates that role through the **flesh** of Christ is new or relatively recent and is a living road; again suggesting this living way is Christ himself.

One of the earliest Christian writings begins with the following: "There are two ways, one of life and one of death: and great is the difference between the two ways."[32] Once again, the passage could be translated as "there are two roads." One of these roads leads to life, the other to death. In *Deuteronomy* 30 we hear, "I have set before you today life and prosperity, death and adversity" (Deut. 30:15). We obey the Lord by walking in the ways of the Lord!

How do we get on that royal road? This road is the thoroughfare of trust! This road is particularly helpful to us who are natural worriers. It is wonderful if you tend to be on the pessimistic or fatalistic side. I am a poor sleeper. I find it hard to fall asleep and to stay asleep. When I would be worried about something, it was customary for me wake in a cold sweat. Such was the case recently. A few months ago I retired from regular parochial ministry and moved all my files from my office. Among these files were some very important documents. After a time, I needed one particular set of papers. I could not find them. I was so worried. What was I going to do? It would cause a grave inconvenience if I couldn't discover their whereabouts. I went around with a pain in the pit of my stomach as I looked through every file I had. My sleep was suffering. I had to get up early, but had only slept about 90 minutes. As I was returning to bed, I heard a voice in my spirit say, "When will you trust me?"

This was a "voice" I had heard for years. I thought if I sincerely trusted God to solve my problem, I might be able to get a few hours of sleep. So I made the decision to trust the Lord. At the time I thought that I would have to search every extraneous folder or papers, but that could wait. I was going to put my trust in God, I was going to test it; I was going to sleep! Still on my way to the bedroom, I looked down and saw a bunch of papers and files on the bottom shelf of a small bookcase. I noticed a file folder. I remember thinking, "This couldn't be it." I had passed by that bookcase every day for months! Opening the folder I saw a number of unrelated documents. I continued to examine the folder. *Eureka!* There were the documents! Such a peace and joy came over me. Of a sudden, I understood the woman who found her lost coin, the parable of the lost sheep, and the prodigal son rolled into one!

What does it mean when we say we trust in the Lord? Let's look at the original languages. There are three or four Hebrew words that are translated as "trust." The range of meaning for these words runs the gamut from confidence to hope, to run to for refuge, and to wait for. The Greek words for "**trust**" also have a range of meaning. Again, we encounter to expect, to hope, to confide (which simply means to place one's faith in), and to convince by argument. This is a wide range indeed.

Trust is both God-talk and very positive self-talk. We tell the Lord that we trust him. Such a proclamation has the immediate effect of realizing half the admonition, "Let go and let God." If we truly trust the Lord, we are "allowing God to be God!" Don't we always do that? I'm sorry to say frequently our intentions get the better of us. That is to say, we not only pray for those who are on our hearts and minds, but often specify the exact way the Lord should answer us. In short, as mentioned before, we often dictate the outcome of our prayers. Positive God-talk, the talk of radical trust, contributes especially when we fulfill the first part of the adage, "Let go!" By not telling God how we want our prayers to be answered, we are "letting go."

This also leads us to positive self-talk. If we trust God, we can develop true assessment of ourselves. As we said earlier, false humility is one of the blocks to Christian joy. During this time of great need, trusting God makes our prayer purer. We continue to lift up people and intentions; we just do not express our desires for and about them, we merely lift them before the Lord. Remember "Trust in the Lord with all your heart, and do not rely on your own insight" (Prov. 3:5).

So let us begin along this royal road, this sacred and holy way. It will be a time of goodbyes and hellos. Be prepared to say goodbye to fatalism. Farewell to anxiety. No more Murphy's law. Be ready for peace; say hello to joy and the power of answered prayer. And all this because we have placed our simple trust in God and have not tried to tell him how and when to answer our prayers. These are perfect for our current situation. This virus has brought anxiety and fear. Trust along the royal road will help us.

Perhaps the most ancient metaphor of the life of the Spirit is that of a journey. We have many aids as we progress along the way, the royal road of the Lord. We have the sacraments, especially the Holy Eucharist, the food that sustains us on the road. We have the Holy Word of God to guide us. And we have the charismatic gifts and the fruit of the Spirit. The fruit of the Spirit is mentioned in the *Letter to the Galatians* (Galatians 5:22-23). The gifts are listed in several places in the Bible. *Romans* 12:6-8 lists roles within the Church: prophecy through mercy. *Ephesians* 4:11 lists five offices in the Church: apostle, prophet, evangelist, pastor, and teacher. We encounter the most exhaustive inventory in *First Corinthians* 12:8-10, which includes gifts, prophecy, tongues, and interpretation of tongues. Take a moment now to read the full catalog of these gifts. Later in Chapter 12 (vv28-30), we encounter more offices and gifts. These are the tools that

God has given his people for help along the royal road. All these gifts are not given to all Christians. Notice that these gifts work together for the unity of the Body. "There is one body and one Spirit, just as you were called to the one hope of your calling, one Lord, one faith, one baptism, one God and Father of all, who is above all and through all and in all" (Eph. 4:4-6). I think this is one of the most beautiful passages in the whole scripture. It bespeaks the unity of God's mystical Body on earth; a body bivouacked here and now—to be united permanently in the heavenly Kingdom. So these gifts and offices, while plural, form a unity of the only plan of salvation! Sheltering in place cannot break this unity. It cannot be marred by having to assist at Mass in live streaming. It cannot be eroded by close quarters.

This royal road is bordered by the flora the Bible calls the fruit of the Spirit: "Love, joy, peace, **patience**, **kindness**, generosity, faithfulness, gentleness and **self-control**" (Gal. 5:22-23). These are attitudes all believers need to journey the royal road. There are some interesting differences between gifts and fruit. First notice that the charismatic gifts are plural—even though they work together to build up the Body. The nine elements of the fruit are considered as one. The fruit is singular, letting us know that every believer needs each part for this variegated produce. Like most produce, fruit begins in seed form. We must also note that fruit is the reproductive part of the plant, the part of the plant that propagates its DNA, that which spreads its spiritual influence abroad. So first, the fruit of the Spirit begets more fruit of the Spirit. This is true within our own spiritual gardens, but also among the Christian community. If we gather with people who manifest this fruit, we might well increase the influence of the fruit, the Christian attitude among the people of God to show forth love and joy and peace.

So let's summarize. God has called us to a royal road to progress to greater and greater intimacy with God. He has called us and equipped us all that we may follow him along the way of salvation. We need to approach the Lord Jesus in total and radical trust. We come to him without agenda. We only seek what God wants for our loved ones and us. We know that when we trust God radically, we will never come away disappointed. Then we make true progress in love and joy and peace.

CHAPTER EIGHT

THE WAY, TRUTH, AND LIFE

In a passage regarding the coming of the Messiah, blessed be He, the prophet provides the business card for the Coming One: the blind see, deaf's ears are unstopped, the lame shall leap like a stag! Jesus himself uses those criteria to claim messiah status to John the Baptist. So it is clear this passage refers to Jesus Christ. It is no coincidence that shortly after these references to the miracles of God's anointed is a mention of the way (that is the road)—the royal road:

> A highway shall be there, and it will be called the
> Holy Way; the unclean shall not travel on it, but
> it shall be for God's people; no traveler, not even
> fools, shall go astray. No lion shall be there, nor
> shall any ravenous beast come up on it; they shall
> not be found there, but the redeemed shall walk
> there (Is. 35:8-9).

Where shall this Holy Way be located? It is in the desert. It spans the desert of our sorrows and isolation. It crosses the wilderness of bitter hearts and depression. It even traverses the fear and uncertainty that currently plague the world. This royal road traverses the emptiness of serious illness, the polarization of today's politics—even the horror, drugs, and violence. Yes, this Holy Way, the royal road, leads God's people from fear and bondage, from sin and idolatry. And we must always remember that one of the original names for Christianity was "the way."

Our journey is not only for joy. We crave the fruit of the Spirit, all nine varieties. There is no joy without love, no love without patience. After all, we want all that God has stored up for us: salvation, charismatic gifts, and the fruit of the spirit. And we must remember that the fruit of the Spirit is presented and contrasted with the works of the flesh. The passage from the *Letter to the Galatians,* which speaks to the works of the flesh and the fruit of the Spirit, begins with notion that we are in a battle for life. The flesh is opposed to the Spirit. To better understand the provision for the wayfarer take a moment now and read *Galatians* 5:16-26.

In one of my pastorates we had three charismatic prayer groups. One of the groups was not really employing the gifts. Prophecy and words of knowledge were very uncommon. Even with the lack of charismatic gifts, that particular prayer group often demonstrated love, joy, peace, and the other fruits of the Spirit. Side by side with the first group was another prayer group that demonstrated all the gifts, including praying and singing in tongues. But they did not show love, joy, and peace—the fruit of the Spirit.

Three chapters in *First Corinthians* deal with the prayer meeting. Chapter 12 treats the charismatic gifts; chapter 13 puts the gifts in perspective; and chapter 14 deals specifically with tongues, prophecy, and orderly worship. No Christian is ignorant of the great, soaring beauty of *First Corinthians 13*. What is so special about chapter 13? It is read at weddings and funerals. It praises the primacy of love. The significance of chapter 13 is that it comes right after chapter 12 and right before chapter 14. In other words, it puts love at the center of the Christian experience. This is in keeping with the great commandment (Mark 12:29-31). This love is not a love of affection or emotion; it is rather a matter of the will.

As pastor, it fell to me to try to set things straight. It was a dual mission: to build on the good fruit of the one group, by introducing them to the charismatic gifts. The other group had to be introduced the fruit of the Holy Spirit. Because of a rebellious nature in the second group, I did something I never wanted to do. I suppressed the group. People were jockeying for leadership. What was the remedy? A seventeen-week life in the Spirit seminar! But how would I begin? The morning of the day that the first session of the seminar was to begin, I had a funeral. It was a tragic service for a little infant, barely two weeks old. Little Gabriel had a rare disease called idiopathic arterial calcification, a condition that causes arteries and some internal organs to solidify.

I was already concerned about how I would begin the seminar. The faith-filled parents were bearing up under all of this sorrow. They participated fully in the planning for the sad occasion. I kept praying for the family and for the seminar I had to begin later that evening. The parents requested an extra reading to be read after the Mass. The family released butterflies at the end of the Mass! Simultaneous with this release, the parents chose a reading from *Romans*. Had I known about the royal road then, so much anxiety and worry could have been avoided. The reading was as follows:

> Let your love be genuine; hate what is evil, hold fast to what is good; love one another with mutual affection; outdo one another in showing honor. Do not lag in zeal, be ardent in spirit, serve the Lord. Rejoice in hope, be patient in suffering, persevere in prayer (Rom. 12: 9-12).

Little Gabriel ministered to a whole community. That passage from the *Letter to the Romans* ministered to the hearts of all who attended the funeral. He also helped the pastor with the perfect theme for the dual task of restoring the suppressed prayer group and building up the other group in their exposure to the charismatic gifts. After calling all those affected by the problems we were encountering with our prayer groups, I explained why I was intervening. We proceeded to introduce and reintroduce the principles of life in the Spirit. Again, this is a proof of *Romans* 8:28: "All things work together for good for those who love God, who are called according to his purpose." With all this, how many of us view the Christian walk as being along a particular route? How many of us believe that we have it our own way toward Christ. I do not think we can overstate the theme song of those who follow their own road. Again, this theme song leads us by "my way," not the way of the Lord, not the road constructed by God for his people to sojourn—the royal road. The singer of the hit song "My Way"[33] is facing his death, the final curtain. Does he look for mercy? Does he seek to make things right with God? Rather, he revels in having his own compass, his own route; he travelled his own road. The lyrics to this self-centered song encapsulate the so-called wisdom of the world. It is a raised fist to heaven. It is a personal affirmation, which challenges the sovereignty of the living God. I know that it seems that I am going on and on about these lyrics, but I believe they are emblematic of the corruption of modern living, as personal pleasure and opinion become central to "liberated" personhood.

The fact is that the Way is not enough. Jesus says, "I am the way, the truth and the life." So we can start out by making pursuing our life goals by our own predilections, or by the way pointed out by the Bible and the Church and traditionally the synagogue. We go back to the *Didache*: there are two ways. My way is one of them. The way of the Lord is the other.

If we are on the wrong way, we must seek to get on the right and only way. Remember that Jesus tells us in *John* 14:6b, "No one comes to the Father except through me." No matter how Prometheus-like we may wish to be, no matter what human fist we want to raise to heaven, none of it will put us on the only royal road to God.

Yet, the right road is not sufficient. We must also walk in the truth! It was not enough for the people of God to be put on the right road. The truth is also necessary. We might ask with Pontius Pilate, "What is truth?" (John 18:38) Truth today is at a premium. People are fired because they make the statement that there are only two sexes. This is something that is patently and demonstrably true, yet the modern mindset rails against this truth. But it is more basic than that. Today ideology has taken the place of truth. St. Paul speaks of this problem when he writes, "The wrath of God is revealed from heaven against all ungodliness and wickedness of those who by their wickedness suppress the truth" (Rom. 1:18). St. Paul continues to remind us that God has made himself known through the natural world. A rejection of the notion of intrinsic, that is, absolute truth is making the scientific method less and less possible. Those who do not side with truth, who ask the same question as Pontius Pilate, bring to modern thought a doctrinal rejection of the possibility of truth—that is, unless it is their own personal subjective truth.

Jesus identifies himself as truth. He is timeless truth. Jesus made his famous statement while he was teaching in the treasury of the temple. The Lord spoke to those Jews who believed in him, "If you continue in my love, you are truly my disciples; and you will know the truth and the truth will make you free" (John. 8:31b-32). The response of these believers in Jesus is a little difficult to understand. They tell Jesus something astonishing: "We are descendants of Abraham and have never been slaves to anyone. What do you mean by saying, 'You will be made free'?" (John 8:33). Either the group with whom Jesus is speaking is thinking in extremely myopic terms or they do not believe the Torah when it says the Jews were slaves in Egypt. On the one hand, they are thinking only of their immediate history, while on the other hand they seem to discount the biblical teaching of the Passover. What Jesus is really saying is that when we sin, we become slaves to sin. We will discuss this in greater detail in the next chapter. For now, we only need to consider the importance of truth along the royal road. Here we do not consider the effect of truth, but only its presence.

Twenty-five percent of the uses of the word "truth" appear in the *Gospel of John.* One the most important occasions in which Jesus speaks of truth takes place in the upper room as part of the high priestly prayer. What the Lord says there is all the more important because it is his farewell address and his final commissioning before his death and resurrection. The entirety of chapter 17 bears reading. So let's put down this book and open our Bibles.

Let me direct you to an important part of chapter 17, particularly important to our progress along the royal road: Jesus says, "Sanctify them in the truth; your word is truth" (John 17:17). What makes this passage most applicable to us is verse 20: "I ask not only on behalf of these, but also on behalf of those who will believe in me through their word" (John 17:20). That is you and me!

We are sanctified in the truth. That is, we are set aside for the Lord. In fact, Jesus, speaking to his Father, says to the apostles and to us: "As you have sent me into the world, so have sent them (the apostles) into the world" (John 17:18). How and for what did God the Father send Jesus into the world? In *Luke* chapter 10, Jesus sent out seventy in pairs as an advance team to everywhere that Jesus was going. Their actions were to heal, to cast out demons, and proclaim the nearness of the Kingdom of God. The true mission of the apostles has not changed: to make disciples of all nations, baptizing them in the name of the Father and of Son and of the Holy Spirit, teaching them to obey all that Jesus taught. He told them to remember that he is with us always to the end of the age. (See Matthew 28:16-20.)

The Lord sends us to bear witness to the truth that Jesus Christ has come in the flesh; that God, beginning with the Torah and ranging through the whole Bible, has revealed Himself to humankind. As we put the truth to work for the Kingdom and ourselves, we must keep in mind that we did not choose God; God chose us. He chose that we should bear much fruit. Jesus is the Way and the Truth. On the royal road, the Lord asks us to live knowing Jesus—as a real living person—not as an abstract principle. Because we trust our Savior we come to know the Truth. But faith and trust are not alone. We must keep in mind that Jesus is also the Life. For us to progress along the royal road, we must apply the truth—in short, we must translate the truth into holy living. In doing so, we become our most authentic self. We experience joy and meaning is our lives and truth in a world that finds it fashionable to have no truth.

CHAPTER NINE

Prayer, Temptation, and Sin along the Road

It should be clear by now that the expression of joy and the notion of the royal road is a way of life and prayer suited for both times of fulfillment and times of distress.

I have been to a number of Science Fiction conventions. These gatherings are always entertaining and diverse. This is true of the topics discussed and the sociology of those who attend. There are many religious and non-religious philosophies and practices represented. On one occasion I was looking over items in the dealer's room. I came upon a blasphemous bumper sticker. It read: "He died 2,000 years ago; get over it."

But we can never get over it. He came among us and is still with us. He died and rose from the dead. And if we know him, nothing will ever be the same again.

Jesus tells us that he is with us to the consummation of the world. For us, temptation and sin along the royal road is different from temptations we've experienced as we're willy-nilly picking our way toward the Lord by any other route. To explore this we must first consider the nature of temptation and the nature of the environment of the royal road. So, are you ready to get off the surface streets, the byways, and back streets? Are you tired of traveling with and toward Christ just doing 25 miles per hour? Are you ready to get on God's freeway, his divine turnpike? Are you ready to move your spiritual life at a speed and with a direction that you never imagined before?

Our prayer changes from telling God what we want, how we want it, and when we want it to recognizing that God knows best what we need for ourselves, our loved ones, and our circumstances. Because we are not stipulating outcomes, we can look everywhere for fulfillment and not miss it because of our spiritual myopia.

We enter the royal road through radical trust. Radical trust manifests itself in abandoning our practice of praying the same prayer over and over again, as if God did not hear us the first time. When we pray for outcomes—that is, exactly what, how, and when we want something to turn out—we run several risks. It is easy for us to say God didn't hear our prayer because he didn't bring something about according to our satisfaction.

Because we don't have a "dog in the fight" we can receive from God, what is best for us in our situation? God desires us to bring our needs to him, but by coming to him along the royal road, we can reduce the anxiety of feeling our prayer is unanswered. In other words, we may not have our prayer answered according to our specific desire and timetable. This can lead to further anxiety, and the notion that God has not heard or answered our prayers. This can lead to a lack of **boldness** before God. This can reduce even bringing our needs to God. Sometimes the usual list of intentions for which we have specific outcomes in mind can limit the activity of the Holy Spirit in our lives.

Prayer of this kind is aided by praying in tongues. We do not really know what we are saying when we pray in tongues; therefore we can perfectly trust that God will act. We lift up the names or circumstances and pray fervently in a tongue. There are several effects from this way of prayer on the way. Once again, anxiety flees. We are encouraged to look all around us for the fulfillment of our prayers. This can result in seeing a lot of good things happening around us. It helps to build our relationship with Jesus because trust begets trust.

Our progress along the Lord's way is based on radical trust—even in temptation. So let's look at the scriptures about the nature of temptation. We think of temptation as an inducement to sin, especially to commit serious sin; yet, much of the time the temptation is merely a test. This is often what happens when adversaries of the Lord Jesus try to trap him. They ask him pointed questions. In *Matthew* 16:1; 19:3; and 22:35, his enemies ask for signs; they test him on the subject of divorce. They pester him about which commandment is the greatest. In the dramatic passage in *John*, chapter 8 they tested him about the woman caught in the act of adultery. Their motive is revealed in verse 6, when they pose the question "in order that might have some charge to bring against him" (John 8:6b). This is one form of temptation.

We also remember the greatest sequence of temptation of the Lord. The Spirit leads Jesus to the desert in order that the devil might tempt him. There is a point of similarity of the Pharisees and Sadducees and the devil: the intention is to destroy Jesus' mission and life in us.

We are usually tempted by the devil. For us the motive is to get us to sin. When we commit serious sin, it disrupts our mission. When we commit mortal sin it destroys our life with Christ. Without the sacrament of reconciliation we incur spiritual death. So in some ways all temptation, whether diabolical or human, is designed to put us down.

But Jesus Christ has come in the flesh! Although he died 2000 years ago, he rose 2000 years ago. And this changed everything—even the notion of temptation. Today we experience some of the same human testing that our first-century brothers and sisters endured. St. Paul says as much to the church at Thessalonica. Paul reminds them he warned them that they would suffer persecution. "For this reason, when I could bear it no longer, I sent to find out about your faith; I was afraid that somehow the tempter had tempted you and our labor had been in vain" (I Thes. 3:5). In today's world, the Christian community is suffering from hostility to outright persecution. Some 260 million people live in places where there is open hostility to Christ and his Church. Last year 2,983 Christians were killed for their faith in Christ; 9,488 churches and other buildings were attacked.[34] So the temptation to leave the faith, coupled with immorality in root and branch and in departure from the ancient teachings of the Church, are very real.

However, most of us think of temptation to personal sin as the primary concern for those following Christ in the Holy Spirit. As the Spirit led Jesus to the desert, the devil tempted the Lord in the areas of hunger, provoking him to prove his divinity by leaping off the parapet of the temple and the greed of power. In each case, the devil quotes scripture. Jesus counters the temptation in his strength and the authority of the sacred scriptures! (Matthew 4:3-11). So, for us, familiarity with God's word is an important part of our resisting the snares of Satan. As we will see when we approach temptation, Jesus is with us. Before we discuss this singular grace, we must look at the environment of the royal road.

Although the royal road is a metaphor, it is quite real. When we see ourselves on this royal road in the power of the Holy Spirit, we progress along the way—even at times a way of suffering and sacrifice—yet one in intimate union with the Lord and our brothers and sisters! Let us consider the environment of the royal road. First Jesus tells us:

> Enter through the narrow gate; for the gate is
> wide and the road easy that leads to destruction,
> and there are many who take it. For the gate is
> narrow and the road is hard that leads to life, and
> there are few who find it (Matthew 7:13-14).

It would be tempting to interpret this passage as a countering the notion of a royal road. But a reading of the original language and comparison to other scriptures supports the view of the prophet Isaiah. Let's look at *John* chapter 10. Jesus tells us that he is the gate. Whoever enters by Jesus will be saved and will come in and go out and find pasture (see John 10:9). The words "narrow gate" refer in general to a gate in a city wall. The gate to life is narrow because it goes against our inclinations to doing it according to our own ideas. It is "narrow" because it is doesn't validate every notion of God and each opinion of what constitutes morality. That is why I condemn the sentiments expressed in the song "My Way." That could be interpreted as "My Road." The road is a royal road precisely because it is the road of the King, the way of the Shepherd. While Jesus indicates the road to life to be narrow and hard, he tells us that his yoke is easy and his burden is light (see Matthew 11:29-30). On the surface it looks like there could be a conflict between various views of the royal road to life.

Yet the very terrain of this spiritual way of the Lord goes to explain and harmonize what can seem contradictory. To help us with this enigma, we turn to St. John Chrysostom (349–407). He tells us, "Does it not seem inconsistent then to say here that the good road is narrow and constricted? Pay attention. He has made it clear the burden is very light, easy and agreeable. 'But how,' one may say is the narrow and constricted road easy?' Because it is both a gate and a road."[35] He goes on to explain that the other road is also a gate and road, but the road leads to eternal sorrow!

So temptation on the royal road is not as direct as it is on the self-chosen meandering pathways of the world where there are crossroads, dead-ends, and dangerous neighborhoods with wild beasts and every kind of inducement to sin. By contrast, the royal road is direct. On the royal road, Jesus is especially our yokemate. The road may not be easy, but our immediate company is with Christ. We can hear the sirens call, we can imagine the inducement to lust, but they are more remote from us. Nothing unclean may walk on this road!

Why do temptations seem less when we envision ourselves on the royal road? Partly because our eyes are fixed on the road, which is Jesus. Our eyes are watching for points along the way, which are the person of the Lord. And as mentioned earlier, since the unclean cannot enter this road, the temptations are more remote from our path and journey. To be sure we will still be aware of them; they can lure us, but because the metaphor of the road is strong, we know we would have to leave the royal road in order to give in to them; we weigh the consequences more carefully. Admittedly, progress along this road requires trust in Jesus. It also benefits from envisioning ourselves as travelling by this road.

If sin seems different when we are on the royal road, it is because we cannot sin while traversing this sacred road. Remember, nothing unclean can use this road. The sacrament of reconciliation plays a large role among our provisions for this walk. When we do sin, sorrow for sin is amplified. We cannot wait to get back on the road. On this road we experience joy and peace. When we leave the road—even for a moment—we lose both joy and peace. This walk is also not a solitary walk. Certainly we walk with Jesus! Since he is the road, truth and life, we walk through him, with him and in him. But we also walk with others. So it is also a journey of fellowship.

CHAPTER TEN

JOY AND THE PRAYER MEETING

As director of the English-speaking charismatic renewal in the Diocese of Oakland, California, I have had the privilege of visiting many prayer groups. I hoped to encounter abounding joy. In fact over the years I challenged my parishioners to show joy. People coming forward to receiving Communion often presented faces suggesting everything from a gastric condition to the loss of everything, including options and even hope. For years I preached about the joy in the Lord—as if people weren't carrying heavy burdens. So when I spoke about joy, I would always acknowledge these heavy burdens and problems. I would tell them the truth that the joy of the Lord is stronger than all these crosses we carry. I would sometimes relate the story of motivational speaker Leo Buscaglia (1924–1998). He would ask his audience several times, "Are you happy?" The crowd would shout, "Yes!" After Buscaglia carefully led the crowd to a thunderous affirmative, he quietly would admonish, "Tell your face!"

This was my approach before I realized I was asking the difficult, if not impossible: You can't manifest what you don't have. Joy sometimes manifests as a smiling face; for others, joy reveals itself in tears. At that time, I didn't know about the royal road. I was aware only intellectually that joy is a fruit of the Spirit. I actually thought if we were able to raise our eyebrows and cheekbones and turn up the corners of the mouth that we would be able to achieve the appearance of joy; the lead of the physical body would inevitably lead our spirit to joy. I was wrong! I was wrong for at least three reasons: disposition, emotion, and spirit.

Christian joy is not a natural disposition to cheerfulness. In my experience this is unusual. Many of us act like Eeyore, the pessimistic donkey from A. A. Milne's *Winnie-the-Pooh*. Eeyore always looks on things on the gloomy side. With a sigh he says, "I'm just an old gray donkey." It seems that the disposition of this beloved character was naturally pessimistic, by nature filled with woe. What's more, Eeyore seems to enjoy his negativity; it is his nature. Less frequently, we encounter those who always appear cheerful—no matter how dire or challenging a situation they may experience. A dear friend of mine was driving with white knuckles on a two-lane highway with an 800-foot drop, and she merely said, "We're on an adventure!" So we must remove natural disposition from Christian joy, whether one is susceptible to gloom or perpetually upbeat. Either of these two extremes is hard to live with. These natural inclinations can cause problems, especially during times of tribulation.

Joy is not an emotion based on circumstances. It is deeper than happiness. Just as the Lord beckons us to choose life, to value Christian love (*agape*), to be perfect as the Father is perfect, not from things going our way, not from some kind of naïve faith in mankind. Psalm 118:8 reminds us: "It is better to take refuge in the Lord than to put confidence in princes." The princes of this present day are political leaders along with their much-vaunted "isms." We must look only to the Lord for vindication and therefore for our joy. So true joy is not dependent on our physical well-being. It is a sign of the grace of God, his loving **hesed** for us, which is the cause of joy.

Joy is a fruit of the Spirit. The Bible touches on this fruit in chapter 5 of the *Letter to the Galatians*. Joy, among the rest of the fruit of the Spirit, is a touchstone of spiritual warfare! The flesh is at odds with the Spirit. It would be tempting to ask how to receive the fruit of the Spirit. The principle established in *Mark* 4:26-28 applies to the fruit of the Spirit. It sprouts and grows. The fruit of the Holy Spirit is given to all who are truly following Christ. But fruit does not appear full grown. So there is nothing to do to receive this fruit. One must believe and be baptized. One needs to receive Baptism of the Holy Spirit. The maturation of this fruit is aided by taking the royal road.

How can we help the fruit the Lord has already planted in us to mature? Let's look at the charismatic prayer meeting. Returning to my visitation of prayer groups, there are five areas that can build or deconstruct the growth medium for the precious fruit: music, word gifts, healing, deliverance, and fellowship.

Most prayer groups under my care are in great shape. They are oases of the fruit of the spirit, especially joy. In my visitations, the main theme of those groups that seem short on joy and enthusiasm seems not to be participating in actual charismatic prayer. A general outline of the prayer meeting is found in *First Corinthians,* 11. We have very little guidance for the use of music in the prayer meeting. St. Paul admonishes us to be "filled with the Holy Spirit as you sing **psalms**, and **hymns** and **spiritual songs** among yourselves, sing and making melody to the Lord with your hearts…" (Eph. 5:18b-19). A parallel passage in *Colossians* says even more about the importance of song in prayer. "Let the word of Christ dwell in you richly; teach and admonish one another in all wisdom; and with gratitude in your hearts sing psalms, hymns and spiritual songs to God" (Col. 3:16). A few things are apparent from these passages: Music is a command, an imperative from and for God. Singing is usually associated with joy.

- Psalm 5:11, "But let all who take refuge in you **rejoice**; let them ever sing for joy."
- Psalm 9:2, "I will be glad and exult in you; I will sing praise to your **name**, O Most High."
- Psalm 51:14, "Deliver me from bloodshed, O God, O God of my salvation, and my tongue will sing aloud of your deliverance."
- Psalm 59:16, "But I will sing of your might; I will sing aloud of your steadfast love in the morning."
- Psalm 63:7, "For you have been my help, and in the shadow of your wings I sing for joy."

Finally *James* asks, "Are any among you suffering? They should pray. Are any cheerful? They should sing songs of praise"

(James 5:13). Deliverance is one reason and effect of singing. We rejoice because God is our refuge, and we sing of it. We sing loudly of God's steadfast love (*hesed*). In music we can hide in the shelter of God's protection. This is a shelter in every sense of the word.

That being said, how does our music, especially in the prayer meeting, feed our joy in the Lord? Music is an architectural feature of Christian joy. The least joyful meetings I have attended either lacked music altogether or used it sparingly. One or two verses are seldom enough. The joy is proportionate to the amount and vigor of the music. For those less familiar with music in charismatic prayer, there are two main varieties of singing: praise and worship. The opening songs should be lively, but not too lively. People often begin the meeting a little tired from the workday. But praise music should build both in tempo and volume. To achieve this end, repetition plays an important role. The chief fault is music that is too slow, too short, and too routine. So one way to experience more joy in the prayer meeting is to amplify the song. One of the best emotional and spiritual investments for prayer groups looking for a deeper walk with Christ is to find and keep musicians. Singers and players on the royal road need to understand the shape of the prayer meeting and the catalog of praise and worship music. Incidentally, music based on Israeli folk songs makes great praise music—especially those tunes that get faster and faster as each verse is sung or repeated.

At various times, during the various praise songs, there should be a time of spoken praise, what we might call resting praise. Sometimes these rest areas along the royal road are for praying or singing in tongues. At some point in the meeting the music will become deeper and quieter. This leads into actual worship. The singing in tongues becomes broader and more fervent. Eventually this should give way to profound silence. This silent is loaded with joy and peace. So, in my opinion, the first triage for a less-than-joyful prayer group should be around music!

A second area of groups with less joyful attendees might be because many people have not been baptized in the Holy Spirit. I have attended some prayer meetings that were primarily a Bible study. I actually attended one that featured some violent chapters of the Old Testament. Nor was there anyone present with a sufficient knowledge of the Bible to make too much sense out of the passage. Music had been from a recording. The people were very nice, but there were no word gifts. My conclusion was that although those in attendance were very kind people, it was not a charismatic prayer group. The word gifts were not practiced, and there was no singing or praying in tongues. The remedy for this situation is to capitalize on the good feelings and kindness of the group and their willingness to participate in a Life in the Spirit Seminar.

The one very strong component this group had was their fellowship and love for one another. Fellowship is very important to growth in Christ. The royal road is not a solitary walk. However, we uncommonly walk as families. Most of us are married, but how often are we on the royal road together? Most of us don't even have meals together. This is one reason why Paul warns about being unequally yoked with unbelievers (2 Cor. 6:14). The word **yoke** has many meanings in the New Testament: there is the yoke of Jesus, a yoke of slavery, a yoke of marriage, and several other uses of the word. Jesus invites us to take his yoke upon ourselves and learn of him. He is meek and humble of heart. Doing so will give us rest (Matthew 11:29). To walk on the royal by ourselves is not possible; Jesus leads us and walks with us. Jesus has at least fifty names and titles. Two stand out: Son of God and Son of man. I believe he reveled in the title of Son of man, because in that role he was down close to us; that is, he was meek and humble of heart. He joins himself to us; his yoke joins us to him (Matthew 11:29). But notice that we must take his yoke upon us. We must see ourselves yoked to Jesus. By analogy he is the experienced draft animal; he leads us, the inexperienced, safely and joyfully along the royal road.

So we are not alone on the royal road; the Lord is with us, yoked to us.

Another sense of the word "yoke" is that of marriage, the joining of man and woman. Imagine what can be accomplished in prayer and practical Christian living if couples already yoked in the Lord felt that they were yoked on the highway of the King! You would be pulling in the same direction, noticeably joined by Christ Jesus. Too often, the woman may recognize the beauty of being a couple on the royal way, yet the husband is not with the program. This does not mean only things like Mass attendance, church leadership, and such. It is also a day-to-day traveling along the road of salvation. Such yoking sends us forth to share Christ with others, while it provides a haven to return to at the end of the workday.

We may also envision journey of the way as pilgrimage. We should present this as an adventure to our children. This adventure does not have an 800-foot drop. One of the important things in bringing the kids on this way is that we must show and tell. We show our kids that Jesus is real, alive, and leading us. We can trust the Lord that he will equip us to be good parents, caring and providing for the physical well-being of our families; we must also introduce them to Jesus, the Way, Truth, and Life. All good Christian parents know the importance of this, but still our children are being snatched away from the faith, abducted from trust in Jesus. The parent therefore needs to share powerful witness to Jesus. Let them see you pray together, especially at Mass. Prepare them by studying the scriptures for Mass each week. Above all, introduce them to Christ through your own Christ-like actions. We need to remember that the royal road is not something we journey just on Sundays or at prayer or at leisure. It is a way from which we do not depart—even when we are at work, shopping, going to school, or enjoying recreation. One secret to staying together on this route of salvation is to show that we are journeying with Jesus.

We must also tell them everything they need to know. Before their teen years, our children must know Jesus personally, and to be able to explain why Jesus makes a difference in their lives. St. Peter admonishes us, "Always be ready to make your defense to anyone who demands from you an account of the hope that is in you; yet do it with gentleness and reverence" (I Peter 3:15b). Recently at a parish fish fry our seminarian and I fielded a question from a fellow fish eater. He was not a believer.

He wondered if he had committed a social faux pas by asking what faith in Christ accomplished for various people at the fish fry. He was yelled at. After all, it was none of his business. The fruit of the Spirit—especially joy—helps us to have a response when asked such questions. No matter how young our children, they will have their faith challenged in schools and universities; they must know Jesus and know why it is sensible to believe and trust in him.

The joy we experience along the way is eternal and strong. It is protective from despair and defeat. Our fellowship helps us to live the life of Christ. The Holy Spirit leads us strongly to Christ. We know we are on the royal road in the Spirit with the charismatic gifts and the fruit of the Holy Spirit, completely equipped for a life of humble trust in Jesus, through him, with him, and in him.

CHAPTER ELEVEN

WALKING THE ROYAL ROAD IN TIMES OF WORLDWIDE CHALLENGE

As I write this meditation, I am sheltering in place. For most of us it seems that the world has changed totally. Until a few days ago, my life was bound by the calendar: Mass at certain times, meetings and counseling. For countless others of you, there was a certain routine that prevailed until a couple of weeks ago. You got up to go to work, probably gulped something hot. If you are an organized person, you said your morning prayers and ate breakfast. Children were awakened, bathed, and prepared for the mad rush to the car for school. There were concerts and weddings and funerals and kiddie birthday parties and after-school sports. There was the anticipation of sports seasons and hockey playoffs. There was daily Mass and reception of the Holy Eucharist.

Now funerals are restricted to graveside services; weddings are postponed, looking toward better days to come. If you are a frequent flier, you are grounded; if you coach student sports, you are on a time out of undetermined length. If you run a "non-essential" business, you find yourself on an unseasonal vacation. There is no business as usual! In all of this, aren't you glad that Jesus Christ is the same today, yesterday, and forever? (Heb. 13:8)

Recently our Bishop ordered public Masses to cease for the time being. The priests in this house concelebrated Sunday Mass at the dining room table, separated by about six feet. I'm getting ready to go outside and hear drive-through confessions. As of this writing, the sheriff has put an end to that! The whole of life has changed! The coronavirus has brought the world to its knees. In this unprecedented worldwide event we are called to look at the world in a profoundly different way.

This microscopic enemy of humankind is no stranger to the Holy Church throughout the world. For those who have a tendency to reject "organized religion," we must keep in mind the experience of Saul of Tarsus (later St. Paul) on the road to Damascus (Acts 9:1-19). A light from heaven flashed and he fell to the ground. Saul heard the voice saying, "Saul, Saul, why do you persecute me?" Saul asks the voice who he is. The reply, "I am Jesus, whom you are persecuting" (Acts 9:5b).

This unambiguous declaration on the part of Jesus is a great comfort in this distressing hour. First, the truth is that the Church is the Body of Christ. When the voice asks Saul, why does the Jewish leader persecute him, he doesn't say: "Why are you persecuting my people?" Instead, he makes it clear than in oppressing the Church, he is oppressing the Lord! This is in keeping with Jesus' promise, "And remember, "I am with you always, to the end of the age" (Matthew 28:20). In *Hebrews,* Jesus tells us, "I will never leave you or forsake you" (Heb.13: 5b). The writer of Hebrews adds the following hope-filled words: "So we can say with confidence, *The Lord is my helper; I will not be afraid. What can anyone do to me*"? (Heb. 13:6). The words in italics are from Psalm 118:6.

So those are the first thoughts of comfort from our Lord, to help us get through tough times. But as the commercials say, "But wait, there's more!" Notice that Jesus doesn't answer Saul's question by saying any of the following: "It is the Lord; it is the Lamb of God; it is the Son of Man." No. He uses his personal name. The name given him by the Angel is used. What does that mean to us as we face the worst pandemic of modern times? It means that it is Jesus, himself, the one who was born at Bethlehem, who taught in Galilee and Judea, who visited Pagan regions, who died at Jerusalem and rose from death—it is he, Jesus, the God-Man who promises to be with us always, and that in some mystical way, we are his Body! That is one reason that why having a personal relationship with Jesus is so important. The journey along the royal road is based on trust in Jesus as Lord and Savior. So even in time of sheltering in place, in isolation, we are never alone! For some people like me, this is not different from usual; except for dinners with parishioners and friends, the social realities haven't changed much. It is for families that sheltering in place provides some of the biggest challenges to confinement and family life itself. We will discuss this a little later in this meditation.

For now our point is that although the novel COVID-19 is unprecedented, it is not so for the 2000-year-old Church! The Church has been on the front lines of pandemics in recorded history. The Church has not only witnessed but also played a large role in alleviating some of the greatest pandemics of the last two millennia. The Antonine Plague raged between 165 and 180 AD. This plague might have killed off 25% of the Roman Empire, but it also led to an increase in the number of Christians. Christians cared for the sick; they also gave testimony to the plague not as the punishment of capricious Olympian gods but as the result of a creation in revolution against the loving God.

In 249 AD another pandemic ravaged Rome and its far-flung Empire. The Plague of Cyprian was named after the Bishop of Carthage (c. 200–258 AD), who first described the outbreak. At its height, the epidemic killed about 5,000 people each day in the City of Rome. The Roman army was decimated by the pestilence. The demise of paganism paralleled that of Roman troops. The Christians exhibited charity and kindness to the victims, Christians and Pagans alike. Know that at the time of the Cyprian Plague, the Church was also being brutally persecuted. In 311 AD, *The Edict of Toleration* theoretically ended the persecution. The *Edict of Milan* (313 AD) made it possible for the Christian Church to recover her property and to operate publically.

One of the unforeseen results of Christians ministering to plague victims was a huge rise in interest in Christians and Christ himself. Decades later, the Emperor Julian responded to the Christian response to the plagues. He threw off the Christian faith and sought to build a kind of response force within paganism. While Julian repudiated the faith, he also blamed Christian behavior during the plagues. It was Christian benevolence to strangers and taking care of the graves of the dead that stood out. "The impious Galileans" took care of their own, and those who didn't believe in Christ.

The Church is no stranger to the terror of plagues and pandemics. Some of the response of the Church to these pandemics was the same as it is in the present day. St. Charles Borromeo (1538–1584), Bishop of Milan suspended the celebration of Mass in its usual context—that is, in church buildings. He celebrated the Mass outdoors so that people could hear and see the Mass.

Much of the religious response to the Black Plague, which killed as much as two-thirds of the population of Europe, was the local patron saint. You may want to go online to check out these plague saints. Saints Sebastian and Rosalia, and especially St. Roch or Rocco, are compelling.

What is in our spiritual survival kit? Strangely enough, the walk along the royal road is a basic direction for not only survival but for soaring in the Spiritual life. Remember, it is a walk with Jesus himself, along a road that is Jesus himself. He is the way, the truth, and the life! It is important for our peace of mind to shelter in place and to follow whatever other directives we receive from authority during these challenging times. This is what Christians do; listen to St. Peter: "For the Lord's sake accept the authority of every human institution, whether the emperor as supreme, or of governors as sent by him to punish those who do wrong and to praise those who do right. For it is God's will that by doing right you should silence the ignorance of the foolish. As servants of

God, live as free people, yet do not use your freedom as a pretext for evil (I Peter 13-16). So a good remedy in the spiritual toolkit is not to complain because of the inconvenience.

We might even look on detention as an opportunity to spend time together, uninterrupted by conflicting schedules and work commitments. For a family, you finally have time together! Try to make a real adventure of it. If you are homeschooling for the first time, this can be a real exciting and perhaps daunting venture. Shared movies, stories read together, and family prayer are sure-fire activities. I also highly recommend "99 Essential Gregorian Chants" on YouTube! As I have said before, even 15 minutes of this heavenly music each day is guaranteed to fill your living space with peace. For couples, this can be a great time to strengthen your relationship. It is often hard for men to express their emotions verbally; this is a great time for you to learn writing daily love notes to each other. This may feel awkward at first, but it can help couples to get along better when cooped up.

I have no family near me. I am used to being alone; but ministering to individuals and families usually offsets this. For folks like myself, there are a few more measures that fill out the paraphernalia in our spiritual toolkit. First, make sure you phone friends and family, and people in ministry, to visit and share and pray together. This will cheer and encourage both sides of the conversation. It will also have the advantage of strengthening our friendships later on when this whole thing is over.

I always lament that I do not have time to tidy my room. Now I have time to do so. I've never had enough time to write, but now I do. Our lives can slow down a little from the marathon pace we usually maintain. Finally, through all of this we might wish to begin a special novena. Fr. Don Dolindo Ruotolo (1882–1970) composed the Novena of Surrender to the Will of God. It is based on a prayer of trust. The prayer is: "O Jesus, I surrender myself to you, take care of everything!" You can find the novena on catholicdoors.com.

May the Lamb of God lead us to the true springtime of salvation through this desolate winter. May our efforts to walk the royal road of the Lord bear fruit in eternity. We have been told to shelter is place. We Christians need to shelter in Grace! "You who live in the shelter of the Most High, who abide in the shadow of the Almighty, will say to the Lord, 'My refuge and my fortress; my God in whom I trust'" (Psalm 91:1). May God richly bless you now and forever.

GLOSSARY

This glossary is certainly not exhaustive. It is intended to give the gist of what the original languages denote. At the same time, changes in meaning in the English language affect the subtle means of much of sacred scripture. The numbers included with the words are Strong Numbers. These are included because they have become a leading part of doing methodical word studies. First published in 1890, *Strong's Concordance* assigned a number to every word in the English Bible. He also included two lexicons in which these numbers defined and clarified the meaning of the words in Hebrew and Greek. These numbers have been provided to encourage you to further study. An H or a G in front of the number indicates the Hebrew or Greek lexicon. Pronunciation is set aside with brackets. Other resources have been used in preparing this glossary.[36]

Anxiety: H-8424 תּוּגָה [too-gaw]. This word is used in the Old Testament for depression or anxiety. It literally means heaviness, as in heaviness of heart. It comes from another Hebrew root, H-3013 יָגָה [yaw-gaw]. It means to be sad, weighed down, or grieved. We also encounter another word, G-3308 μεριμνα, translated as anxiety. It means to be distracted or to be drawn in different directions. Another important word is G-3077 λυπη [lup-ay]. It means sadness and sorrow. Also, we have G-85 αδημονέω, which means to loathe, to be in distress of mind. These words are used when Jesus enters the garden of Gethsemani. To appreciate the depth of the words for grief and anxiety, we have only to look at Jesus as he prays to the Father, the night he was arrested. Jesus began to be "grieved and agitated." *Matthew* 26:37b-38a might be translated as follows: "And [he] began to be sad and filled with loathsome anxiety. Jesus said, "Distress surrounds me."

Finally, anxiety comes to English from the Latin *anxietatem* from *anxius,* meaning "uneasy or troubled in mind." This word also carries the notion of choking or squeezing.

Boldness: H-982 בָּטַח [béh-tahk]. First, words translated as "boldness" or "bold" are few in the English Bible. This is especially true in the Old Testament, where there are only three uses of words related to "bold." בָּטַח has the basic meanings of trust and confidence. Variations on the word "bold" are also limited in the English Bible. There are only thirty-two instances of five words translated as bold. G-2292 θαρρέω [thar-rhéo] There are two instances of this word, meaning to be of good courage; the root of the word has the notion of warmth. This would be the opposite of "having cold feet." G-3954 παρρνσια [par-rayn-sia] means "to speak freely, to speak plainly." This is the very word used in Hb. 4:16. "Let us therefore approach the throne of grace with boldness, so that we may receive mercy and find grace to help in time of need."

Flesh: H-1320 [baw-sár]. The basic meaning of the word is flesh of meat. Strangely, it is thought to come from another word that means freshness. 1. It can mean the edible part of the body of an animal, the flesh meat excluding bones and blood. 2. This word can also relate to a family relationship, as in "flesh of my flesh and bone of my bone." 3. "All flesh" carries with it the understanding of all humanity. Frequently there is a negative connotation to this word. 4. Sometimes the Bible uses this word to represent illicit sex. But the word also has a more noble meaning as given in *John* chapter 6. "My flesh is food indeed (John. 6: 54 *ad passim*). This application likely comes from the flesh of sacrifice. G-4561 σαρξ [sarx] in Greek signifies the meat of an animal, a direct translation from the Hebrew. 5. Sarx can mean the human body as opposed to the human spirit. Finally, by figure of speech (synecdoche) flesh can signify the human being, body, soul, and spirit. Wow, that is a wide meaning.

Gentleness: H-6031 [aw-náw]. This word is used only twice in the Old Testament as "gentleness." It has the main meaning of "meekness," based on a root that means "looking down." The most famous Old Testament quote using "gentleness" may be from *Proverbs* 15:1: "A gentle answer turns away wrath" (NIV). However, most translations use different words for "gentle," everything from "soft" (KJV) to "mild" (Rheims Douay, 1941). H-7390 רַךְ [rak]. This means quiet or meek. We turn to the New Testament for a closer definition of this fruit of the Spirit. There are two words that might be translated as "gentleness": G-1933 and G-4240 επιεκης [ep-ee-i-kace] and πραυτης [prah-oo-tace]. επιεκης means reasonableness, forebearing, and not insisting on the letter of the law. It is used in *Jas.* 3:17: "But the wisdom from above first pure, then peaceable, gentle, willing to yield, full of mercy and good fruits, without a trace of partiality or hypocrisy."

It is a mindset that is at once kind, and quiet, merciful and teachable.

Πραυτης was much used in antiquity. In secular Greek, the word suggests something soothing. It is used of a salve that can soothe an ulcer. Plato in *The Laws* uses the word for a patient asking the doctor to be gentle in treating him. It is also used in a humane element in training a horse. It is often associated with humility (Col. 3:12). It is a docile spirit that helps in learning. Gentleness is sometimes called meekness. As a virtue this word is the center point between anger and apathy.

Gifts: G-5486 Χαρισμα [Char-is-ma]. This word refers to a gift that is undeserved. It involves and as you will see below is related to the word for "grace." G-1435 δωρον signifies gifts for the support of the temple and of the poor. This word is thus used in *Matthew* 15:5; *Mark* 7:11; and *Luke* 21:1-4: Something that is offered.

Grace and joy: G-5485 Χαρις [char-is]. How these two words are related is that "joy" began its career as a word for favor. Grace was the favor that a king would give to whomever he pleased. Often this was associated with a performance of great beauty or graceful movement. Think of the dance of Herodias' daughter, and the gift that Herod gave her, entranced by her dance. Until the time of St. Paul, grace simply meant the grace of an expressive dancer. After that, the meaning took on a more theological meaning. It is the King who shows us his love, and gifts us with communion with him. It is also related to the word *charismata*, which means 'gifts.'

"Grace" relates to "joy" as they share a root: χαρι [khar-ece], which is often translated as grace or favored. Joy translates χαιρω [khai-row]. It is a form of address that begins many ancient letters. It is equivalent to "greetings." G-20 αγαλλιασις [ag-al-lee-asis] and G-21 αγαλλιαω [ag-al lee-ah-oh] are important words translated as rejoice or "to be extremely joyful" or "to jump for joy." See *Luke* 1:14; 10:21; *First Peter* 1:6.

Guard: G-5432 φροθρεω [froo-reh-oh]. The word translated as "**guard**" is a military term that means to set a guard for our hearts and minds that we live the Christian life. This word is often translated as "to keep." Strong points out that this is not external protection, but "inward garrison of the Holy Spirit."[37]

Hesed: See **kindness.**

Image and likeness: H-6754 [tseh-lem] is translated as image, while H-1823 [dem-ooth] is translated as likeness. The Vulgate translates these two words *imaginem* and *similitudinem*. Much has been written about "image and likeness." Generally speaking no one believes that God's image is a physical one. After all, God is spirit. Among classical Jewish thinkers, Philo (20 BCE–50 CE) and Sa'adia Gaon (882 AD–942 AD) teach that image and likeness does not suggest that God has a physical body. They believe that the passage (Genesis 1:27) means that God bestowed upon his new creation a dignity that he didn't give to the creation in general. The repetition of words "image" and "likeness" are a Hebraism, a kind of parallelism that is the use of different words, almost synonyms. Maimonides (1135 or 1138–1204) thought it was consciousness and the power to speak and reason that rendered in us in the image of God. St. John of Damascus (650 AD–750 AD) proposed an interesting idea: image is manifest in intellect and free will, while likeness is manifest in virtue.[38] This is borne out by the fact that God did not create man from nothing, like the rest of the universe, but out of earth itself. Thus mankind is a hybrid being of earth and of spirit. The earthly is embodied resemblance between God the King of the Universe, and man/woman the monarchs of the earth. God's likeness is conveyed by the breath of life, which God breathed into his new creature, which makes possible likeness to God, living the life of the Spirit of God.

Joy: See **grace and joy.**

Kindness: H-2617 חֶסֶד [kheh-sed], *hesed.* This word has three basic meanings: strength, steadfast, and love. It is a matter of loyalty and mercy. It is the general disposition of the Lord to his people. An example of חֶסֶד is found in *Isaiah* 55:3b: "I will make with you an everlasting covenant, my steadfast, sure love for David." *Hesed* is almost never used as human love for God. It is used for God's loving-kindness for his people. It is used for mercy applied to community and family. G-5544 χρηστός [khrase-tós]. This is a fruit of the Holy Spirit. It is not just something that affects our demeanor; it permeates our whole nature.

Messiah: H-4899 [maw-shee-akh] means an anointed person. Normally this would apply to prophets, priests, and kings. When the passage speaks about the Messiah, it refers to the one who is to lead his people to freedom. G-5547 χριστός [khris-tos] is Christ.

Name: H-8034 שֵׁם [shame]. The name is a euphemism for the revealed name of God (see **tetragrammaton**). This is the name that God revealed to Moses at the burning bush (Exodus 3:14) Because Hebrew has no vowels, the word God gives as his name is only a guess. YHWH is the abbreviation of the Hebrew, which means "I am what I am" or some variation of those words. It was erroneously taught in some English Bibles as Jehovah. Piety forbade the use of the name that is revealed in *Exodus* 3:14, so many other ways arose to refer to him. Some ways are Lord, the Almighty, and the Most High. Naming something could also be a sign of dominion over a thing. For example, Adam named all the animals; the Lord gave Adam dominion over all the animals of the earth and sea (Exodus 1:26). In Jesus the notion of name grew, as did access to the person of God.

Patience: G-3115 μακροθυμία [mak-ro-thoo-mía] is literally large, big, or long-tempered. It is patience with circumstances and with people. It is the basis for humility and fellowship. G-5281 ὑπομονη [hupo-mon-áy] has the connotation of forbearance without tooth gritting, but rather cheerful, joyful, and hopeful endurance. *Colossians* 1:11b-12a reminds us: "May you be prepared to endure everything with patience, while joyfully giving thanks to the Father."

Perfect G-5056 τελος [tél-os]. While this word is translated in various ways, the basic meaning of the word is purpose. This word is used to translate a number of misunderstood passages in God's holy word; for example, this word is used to refer to the familiar English term, the end of the world. While τελος can mean the end of something in a series, it more clearly shows a purpose. For example, the end of the world really speaks of the purpose for which the world was made: to be saved by God. Another use of τελος is to indicate being equipped for a purpose. This explains to us the rather daunting scripture (Mt. 5:48). St. Jerome chose the Latin word *perfectum* to translate τελος. The real meaning of this passage is that we need to be fit for a purpose. God is fit for all purposes. We need to copy God in this by being equipped for the purpose to which God has called us.

Prayer: H-8605 תְּפִלָּה [tef-il-law'] is the word most translated as "prayer," especially in the *Psalms*. This word applies to liturgical and non-liturgical prayer. תְּפִלָּה is often used to convey an intro-spection and "is understood to be an introspection that results in bonding between the creature and the Creator, as a child would bond with his/her father."[39]

H-6419 פָּלַל [paw-lal'] is more common in earlier books of the Bible. In the four uses of the intense form, it means to mediate or judge. Intercession is another use of פָּלַל, (see Genesis 20:7). There are several words in Greek that are translated as "prayer." Two of the most important Greek words for prayer, G-4335 and G-4336 προσευχη' [pros-yoó-khay'] and προσευχομαι [pros-yoó-khom-ahee], respectively indicate prayer that is always directed toward God. Finally, G-4352 προσκυνέω [pros-koon-néh-o] is the word for worship. It means to prostrate oneself, to kiss, like a dog licking his master's hand. It is a profound reverence before God.

psalms, hymns, spiritual songs: H-4210 רוּמְזְמ [miz-more]. In fact, the Greek word translated as psalm refers to the act of touching or plucking of the strings of a musical instrument, usually the harp. However, the widespread use of the guitar also qualifies. G-5568, ψαλμός [psalm-ós]; The Greek is just as the Hebrew, music with accompaniment of plucked strings. We are also called to sing hymns. G-5215 'υνος [hym-nos] is a hymn of praise to God, usually accompanied by musical instruments. Finally we have G-5603 ωδη [o-dáy], New Testament songs to the Lord Jesus. This is also a general term for singing. That's why the adjective *spiritual* is used.

Rejoice: H-8055 [saw-mách]. This is a disposition related to the heart and the soul and bright eyes. This is a joy to be shared. Sometimes the wicked rejoice at the afflictions of the righteous. See also **Grace and Joy**.

Self-control: G-1466 εγκράτεια [eng-krát-i-ah]. This word is translated as temperance in the KJV. This might suggest to us that it had mostly and primarily to do with drinking too much. It essentially means to be strong in a thing. One author does not like the translation "self-control," and goes so far as to say that if it is really control of self that we don't really need the Spirit. This seems to be convoluted thinking, as if the Holy Spirit does not partner with us. There is not much to support an exact definition. The word occurs only four times in the New Testament. In the Septuagint (LXX) it occurs many times, but it does not have a moral meaning, rather to "take hold of." Aristotle uses the word as the virtue to restrain desire by reason.

Tetragrammaton: This word is not used in the Bible as a word; it is rather a designation of the name of God revealed to Moses in the burning bush. יהוה [YHWH]. (See **name**).

Way: G-3598 'odós [hah-dós] has the primary meaning of a road or a path. It also can be a means of the achieving something. Also, it was the first title for Christians—that is, people of the way.

Worry: See **anxiety.**

Yeshua: [yesh-u-ah] is the name of Jesus. There is no other name by which we must be saved (Acts 4:12). It is the name above all other name. At that name every knee shall bow in heaven on the earth and under the earth (Phil. 2:10). It is also the name of Joshua in the Old Testament. G-2424 Ἰησους [ee-ay-sóoce].

Yoke: H-5923 עֹל [ole] and H-4133 [moh-taw]. The first of these refers generally to a yoke that one puts on the necks of draft animals so they can pull together, while 4133 refers to the yoke of slavery. G-2218 Ζυγός [zoo-gos] essentially refers to joining any two things together.

ENDNOTES

1 Dietrich Bonhoeffer. Retrieved from goodreads.com/author/quotes/29333/Dietrrich_Bonhoeffer.

2 The visit of Congressman Ryan and his subsequent assassination was the proximate cause of the forced suicide of over 900 people!

3 As every book of the Torah begins with the first word or phrase, Deuteronomy begins with "These are the Words Moses spoke..." D'varim means "words."

4 *The Complete Jewish Bible, notes, p. 1038.*

5 This translation is elusive. See Dahood, Mitchel *Psalms II. Anchor Bible, vol. 17,* p 7.

6 "On Joy and Sorrow," from *The Prophet, Knopf, 1923.*

7 In Greek, A and Ω, alpha and omega; in Hebrew, א and ת, alef and tav.

8 See *King, Cult and Calendar in Ancient Israel: Collected Studies.* p. 26, Shemaryhu Talmon.

9 *Ancient Commentary on Sacred Scripture.* Vol. X, p. 209.

10 Op cit., p. 210.

11 See Glossary.

12 *Ancient Commentary on Sacred Scripture.* Vol. VIII, p.282.

13 biblestudytools.com/bible-study/topical-studies-who-said-comparison-is-the-thief-of-joy.html.

14 Fun versus Joy, retrieved from http://becomeorthodox.org/fun-vs-joy/.

15 *Summa Theologica,* Question 28.

16 Peter Kreeft, retrieved from https://www.peterkreeft.com/topics/joy.htm.

17 *Ibid.*

18 *Leiber, Jerry & Stoller, Mike,* 1968. "Is that all there is?" Sony ATV Music Publishing.

19 Francis Shaeffer, *Escape from Reason,* p. 256.

20 Revaux, Jacques, François, Claude Thibault, Giles & Paul Anka, 1969. Copyright ownership is disputed.

21 See also Mark 15:16 and CCC 1257.

22 The use of the Trinitarian formula, which is to be Baptized in the name of the Father and of the Son and of the Holy Spirit, is the norm for Christian Baptism. The Trinitarian formula is also attested to by the Holy Scriptures and numerous early Christian sources. The *Didache,* (A.D. 70) [7:1], *The Apostolic Tradition 21* (A.D. 215 A.D); Hippolytus of Rome (170-235 A.D.) *Against Praxeas, 26* (216 A.D.); Tertullian (155-220 A.D.). St. Cyprian of Carthage (253); Eusebius of Caesarea (323); St Cyril of Jerusalem (323); St. Athanasius (361); St. Basil the Great (367); St. Ambrose (379); St. Gregory Nazianzus (380); St. Jerome (382); St. Gregory of Nyssa (383); and St. Augustine (400). What a cloud of witnesses!

23 Leo Jozef Suenens (1999) was a leading voice at the Second Vatican Council. Retrieved from http://ccro-msp.org/what-does-the-church-say/.

24 McDonnell, Killian & Montague, George T., eds. *Fanning the Flame: What Does Baptism in the Holy Spirit Have to Do with Christian Initiation?* The Liturgical Press, Collegeville, Minnesota, 1991.

25 Hilary of Poitier. *Tract on Psalms 64:14;* Corpus scriptorium ecclesiasticorum latinorum 22:246.

26 McDonnell, Killian & Montague, George T., eds., op. cit.

27 Cyril of Jerusalem, *Catechetical Lectures,* 18:32.

28 Quoted in Donnell, Killian & Montague, George T., eds., op. cit., location 175, Kindle edition.

29 For lists of these gifts see I Corinthians 12, Romans 12, Ephesians 4, and I Peter 4.

30 Quoted in *Catholic Charismatic Renewal – CCR.org.UK. Retrieved from* ccr.org.uk/articles/pope-tells-priests-run-life-in-the-spirit-courses/.

31 APA, *Stress and Health Disparities,* 2017.

32 W.A. Jurgens. *The Faith of the Early Fathers.* The Liturgical Press, Collegeville, Minnesota, 1970. P. 1.

33 Revaux with English Lyrics by Paul Anka, 1968.

34 Retrieved from opendoorusa.org.

35 *Ancient Commentary on Sacred Scripture.* Vol. Ia, pp. 152-153.

36 TDOT, TDNT, list other sources.

37 *Strong's Greek Dictionary*, p 267.

38 ACCS, vol. I Genesis p. 35.

39 Dr. Eli Lizorkin-Eyzenberg, *Israel Bible Weekly,* November 12, 2017. Retrieved from weekly.isaraelbiblecenter.com/prayer-mean-hebrew/.

BIBLIOGRAPHY

Botterweck, Johannes G., Ringgren, Helmer and Fabry, Heinz-Josef. Translated by David E.

Green & Douglas W. Stott. Vols. 1–15. (2005). *Theological Dictionary of the Old Testament*. Grand Rapids: Wm. B. Eerdmans.

Dahood, Mitchel. (Translated and Notes) "Psalms" (Vols. 1–3). In *The Anchor Bible* (1968-

2008). John J. Collins (General Editor) .Garden City, New York: Doubleday & Co.

Gibran, Kahlil, "On joy and sorrow." *The Prophet* (1923). New York: Alfred A. Knopf.

Holy Bible. *New Revised Standard Version Catholic Edition.* (1989, 1995, 1999). New York: HarperCollins.

Jurgens, W.A. *The Faith of the Early Fathers.* (1970). Collegeville, Minnesota: The Liturgical Press.

Kittle, Gerhard, ed. (Vols. 1–4), Friederich, Gerhard ed. (Vols. 5–9) and Pitkin, R.E. (compiler

Vol.10) *Theological Dictionary of the New Testament* (1942–1976). Translated by Geoffrey W. Bromiley. Grand Rapids, Michigan: Wm. B. Eerdmans.

McDonnell, Kilian and Montague, George T. (editors) *Fanning the Flame: What Does Baptism in the Holy Spirit have to do with Christian Initiation?* (1991). Collegeville, Minnesota: The Liturgical Press.

Oden, Thomas C., (General Editor). *Ancient Christian Commentary on Scripture.* (1998–2005).

(29 vols.) Downers Grove, Illinois: InterVarsity Press.

Rubin, Barry (General Editor). *The Complete Jewish Study Bible.* (1998–2016). Peabody, Massachusetts: Hendrickson Publishers.

Shaeffer, Francis A., *Escape from Reason.* (1968). London: InterVarsity Press.